Zia's Pakistan

Westview Special Studies

The concept of Westview Special Studies is a response to the continuing crisis in academic and informational publishing. Library budgets are being diverted from the purchase of books and used for data banks, computers, micromedia, and other methods of information retrieval. Interlibrary loan structures further reduce the edition sizes required to satisfy the needs of the scholarly community. Economic pressures on university presses and the few private scholarly publishing companies have greatly limited the capacity of the industry to properly serve the academic and research communities. As a result, many manuscripts dealing with important subjects, often representing the highest level of scholarship, are no longer economically viable publishing projects—or, if accepted for publication, are typically subject to lead times ranging from one to three years.

Westview Special Studies are our practical solution to the problem. As always, the selection criteria include the importance of the subject, the work's contribution to scholarship, and its insight, originality of thought, and excellence of exposition. We accept manuscripts in camera-ready form, typed, set, or word processed according to specifications laid out in our comprehensive manual, which contains straightforward instructions and sample pages. The responsibility for editing and proofreading lies with the author or sponsoring institution, but our editorial staff is always available to answer questions and provide guidance.

The result is a book printed on acid-free paper and bound in sturdy library-quality soft covers. We manufacture these books ourselves using equipment that does not require a lengthy make-ready process and that allows us to publish first editions of 300 to 1000 copies and to reprint even smaller quantities as needed. Thus, we can produce Special Studies quickly and can keep even very specialized books in print as long as there is a demand for them.

About the Book and Editor

President Zia is transforming his martial law government into one that resembles the viceregal system of the early days of the country. The change is not to a parliamentary form of government but to one in which the focus of power is in the presidency. The prime minister, cabinet, and parliament will have limited powers, while the newly created National Security Council, dominated by the military, will "advise" the government on matters of international and domestic security.

Zia ruled as chief martial law administrator for nearly eight years. To do so he required the support of key groups in Pakistan to offset other groups that opposed him, such as the People's Party of former Prime Minister Bhutto. This book assesses the support and influence of major interest groups in Pakistan, each of which bears directly on the survivability of the changing Pakistani regime. The authors believe that Zia will be required to develop further the coalition building techniques he has used successfully so far. The absence of the tool of martial law and the presence of an elected parliament will make it more difficult to suppress demands from the urban and rural areas, more essential to maintain a reasonable level of economic growth, more demanding to meet the requirements of the military, and more important to reach some solution to the problem of Afghani refugees.

Craig Baxter, a retired Foreign Service officer who was stationed in South Asia and Africa, is professor of politics and history at Juniata College, Huntingdon, Pennsylvania. His previous works include *Bangladesh: A New Nation in an Old Setting* (Westview, 1984).

Published in cooperation with
the Middle East Institute,
Washington, D.C.

Zia's Pakistan
Politics and Stability
in a Frontline State

edited by
Craig Baxter

Westview Press / Boulder and London

The paper used in this publication meets the requirements of the American National Standard for Permanence of Paper for Printed Library Materials Z39.48-1984.

Westview Special Studies on South and Southeast Asia

Copyright © 1985 by Westview Press, Inc.

Published in 1985 in the United States of America by Westview Press, Inc.; Frederick A. Praeger, Publisher; 5500 Central Avenue, Boulder, Colorado 80301

Library of Congress cataloging in Publication Data
Zia's Pakistan: Politics and Stability in a Frontline State
  (Westview special studies on South and Southeast Asia)
  1. Pakistan—Politics and government—1971- .
2. Zia-ul-Haq, Mohammed. I. Baxter, Craig. II. Title.
DS384.Z53 1985   954.9′105   85-13768
ISBN 0-8133-7113-9

Printed and bound in the United States of America

10   9   8   7   6   5   4   3   2

Contents

Preface

This paper originally was prepared for the Department of State as part of its external research program under a contract of December 3, 1984, between the Department and the Middle East Institute. The views and conclusions contained herein should not be interpreted as representing the official opinion, policy, or views of the Department of State or the Middle East Institute. The project director for the Institute is Philip H. Stoddard, Executive Director; the principal investigator is Craig Baxter of Juniata College, who also served as editor of this volume.

The editor wishes to express his appreciation for the valuable assistance extended by Dr. Stoddard and other members of the Middle East Institute's staff. He also has very much appreciated the cooperation of the authors of the individual chapters who have done exceptionally well not only in the analysis of their topics but in meeting deadlines. It has been collectively useful for us to look back at the first phase of the Zia regime as we look forward to the next phase, which includes an elected legislature.

Craig Baxter

Introduction

Craig Baxter

The martial law regime of General Muhammad Zia ul-Haq in Pakistan is nearly eight years old. It began on July 5, 1977, when Zia and his military associates overthrew the government headed by Zulfiqar Ali Bhutto as prime minister. In lasting so long, it has exceeded the average life of military regimes by a considerable extent.[1]

Zia, at first, declared himself chief martial law administrator and announced that he had taken office only for a brief period of about 90 days in order to calm the nation and hold new elections. Zia took over in a period of turmoil following the March 1977 elections to national and provincial assemblies. The opposition claimed that the voting had been rigged to give Bhutto and his Pakistan People's party (PPP) a majority—or, at least, a majority at the center larger than the PPP was entitled to had the voters been tallied fairly. The opposition, the Pakistan National Alliance, a coalition of seven parties, took to the streets in demonstrations and rioting. Some concessions were won from Bhutto but not the promise to hold elections anew, the irreducible minimum demand of the opposition. Zia's action, while surprising in its timing and source, was not strongly opposed by the people and seems even to have been accepted reluctantly by Bhutto. To many observers, the surprise was that the military had delayed in exercising an arbiter role as the riots expanded. Bhutto had chosen Zia as chief of staff of the army over the heads of several more senior officers, as Zia was felt to be nonpolitical.

Zia thus appeared be a "guardian," in the term of Eric A. Nordlinger, a temporary governor who wished to correct malpractices and deficiencies, in Zia's case in the electoral system.[2] New elections, which were to be held in September 1977, were to be open to all parties (and alliances of parties), including Bhutto and the PPP. But as the time for elections approached, Zia said that he had found a number of irregularities in the government

1

which would have to be corrected before free elections could be held. A period of "accountability" was mandated, and it was inevitable that the person most affected by this accountability process would be the leader of the ousted government, Zulfiqar Ali Bhutto. Among many other irregularities, some of which have been expounded in government papers, Zia discovered that Bhutto may have been responsible for the instigation of the murder of the father of a prominent opposition leader. Bhutto was charged with the crime, and, after a long process, he was convicted, had his conviction upheld by the Supreme Court, and saw a consideration of mercy denied by Zia. Bhutto was hanged on April 4, 1979.

Meanwhile, Zia, who probably did not have a scheme for governing or for realigning Pakistan's political system before he assumed office, developed traits characteristic of another of Nordlinger's categories: the "ruler," who dominates the regime to effect political and socioeconomic change.[3] It was imperative, as Zia saw it, that Pakistan be transformed from a state in which the Western parliamentary system was the ideal—in spite of the number of times it had been subverted in the period since independence in 1947—into one which would be ruled under nizam-i-mustafa (rule of the Prophet). In other words, Pakistan would become an Islamic state. Some steps in that direction had been taken by Bhutto as he faced the angry opposition, including prohibitions on alcohol and gambling, but these were far short of those foreseen by Zia.

The new leader clearly drew some of this inspiration from the religiously conservative party, Jamaat-i-Islami, and that party's founder Maulana Syed Abul A'la Maududi. Maududi, whose ideas have spread well beyond the borders of Pakistan, had written extensively on the form of an Islamic government as he saw it.[4] In its most basic form, the nation would be led by an amir who would be chosen by some form of election from among those who were faithful to Islam, and who would be advised by a majlis-i-shura of faithful persons but would not be bound by its advice.

Such a form of government raises political as well as economic and social questions. For example, is it possible to have political parties in such a system? Is it possible that the faithful might have differing opinions on matters which can be derived from the sunnah (the accepted practice and belief of the Muslim community, based on the Quran and the hadith, the precedents of the Prophet) and from the expounders of Islamic law? If there were differences, would those who differed be guilty of heresy? Such questions have gripped some of Pakistan's Islamic scholars. Yet many political leaders seem quite clearly to want a competitive political system in which parties operate freely and differing views are put before the electorate. Among some, at least, the concept of a parliamentary system has not disappeared, and this provided one basis for the call for a boycott of the February 1985 elections.

Movement toward an Islamic system has meant changes in the economic system, which are described in the following chapters, especially those on the economic groups (John Adams) and the rural groups (Charles H. Kennedy). An interest-free banking system is one goal of the Zia government. In the rural areas (and in the urban as well), conflicting views on Islamic law between Sunni and Shii Muslims have led to verbal conflict and, at times, demonstrations, as these viewpoints are put forth ardently. The chapters mentioned above, as well as that by Robert LaPorte, Jr., discuss these matters.

Some changes in Pakistan's social system have been received with shock by the Western world. Such matters as Islamic punishments for theft and adultery—amputation, whipping, stoning—have been seen both inside and outside Pakistan as signs of a return to an earlier age in which barbarity was perhaps more common than criminal law systems generally accept today. (It should be noted that of the prescribed punishments only whipping has actually taken place.) Challenges to the improvement (as Westerners would see it) in the status of women have been disapproved of by many leading Pakistani women. Perhaps the most unacceptable change is that which equates the testimony of one man with that of two women. It may not be long before the rights given to women under the Family Law Ordinance of 1961, decreed by President Muhammad Ayub Khan, will be modified or withdrawn.

The Pakistani legal system has also undergone great change, not only as a result of martial law, but also with the institution of Islamic, or shariah, law. Martial law changes have included the withdrawal of writ jurisdiction from the courts, a serious challenge to the legal system Pakistan (and India) inherited from the British. This aside, however, the introduction of shariah courts has permitted individuals to appeal to the court system under two forms of law, Anglo-Saxon as modified for Pakistan and the shariah. For example, as Kennedy notes, appeals against land reform are moving forward in the shariah courts, although the program had withstood all tests in the "regular" court system.

This summary cannot cover all of the changes decreed under the present martial law regime. It is not only domestic reformation and internal governance which have occupied the Zia regime but also vast alterations in the international scene. The Soviet invasion of Afghanistan in December 1979 transformed Pakistan's defense requirements drastically. It also brought the United States and Pakistan closer together than they had been at any time since the 1965 war with India. This event had followed the adoption by Pakistan of a foreign policy which attempted to create equal relations with the United States, the Soviet Union, and China. This new policy owed much of its formulation to Bhutto, who was foreign minister under Ayub. Some have seen the Soviet presence in Afghanistan as a prop for the Zia regime in that provincialism has been somewhat muted in the Northwest Frontier Province (NWFP) and in Baluchistan. Also, a feeling exists among some Pakistanis that a disciplined military regime might be the best defense against a spillover into Pakistan.

Zia has also built upon the previously developing relations with the Middle East, pushed strongly by Bhutto. Pakistan has taken a leading role in the Islamic Conference Organization, where Zia has made it clear to the Arabs that he sees the organization as one for all Muslim states, one which should consider positions beyond those which are strictly Arab. For example, he has spoken for the readmission of both Egypt and Iran to the organization, against the opposition of some Arab states.

Under Zia, relations with India, on balance, have improved, although acrimony remains evident as each accuses the other of interference in internal affairs. Nonetheless, both nations have joined the new South Asia Regional Cooperation (SARC), and an Indo-Pakistan joint council has been established. The areas in which these groups can act are severely limited, but their establishment can be seen as progress.

Zia has thus set out to transform Pakistan, a goal which apparently was not his when he assumed office. To do this he cannot rely solely on the coercive power of the military. Indeed, he must also consider the military as a group with a political as well as a security role, one which in the former role might well oppose rather than support him. Zia will not be without opponents, some opposing him on almost all he does or tries to do, others selective in their opposition. Like any political figure he must build coalitions of support, rewarding, stimulating, and even coercing those whose opposition seems dangerous. To use a title from W. Howard Wriggins, Zia must pursue the ruler's imperative, survival.[5]

In this study, a number of interest groups are identified and the level and consistency of their support (or lack of it) for the Zia regime are explored. It is critical to look for possible turning points when supportive groups may turn against the regime, perhaps causing its downfall. We have chosen four longstanding indigenous groups: the urban population (LaPorte), the rural groups (Kennedy), the economic leaders (Adams), and the military (Rodney W. Jones), and to these have added a fifth, new to Pakistan but possibly of long-term consequence: the Afghan refugees (Grant M. Farr).

NOTES

1. See Eric A. Nordlinger, Soldiers in Politics: Military Coups and Governments (Englewood Cliffs, N.J.: Prentice-Hall, 1977), 138-47, for a discussion of the longevity and stability of military regimes. On p. 139, he states that such regimes have an average life span of five years and adds that "it can be said that they are inherently unstable."

2. Nordlinger, Soldiers in Politics, 22.

3. Ibid.

4. Perhaps the standard work available in English is Abul A'la Maududi, Islamic Law and Constitution (Lahore: Islamic Publications, 1955). It was translated by Khurshid Ahmad, who served briefly in Zia's cabinet.

5. W. Howard Wriggins, The Ruler's Imperative: Strategies for Political Survival in Asia and Africa (New York: Columbia University Press, 1969).

Urban Groups and the Zia Regime

Robert LaPorte, Jr.

Background

As of 1982, 29 percent of Pakistan's 87.1 million people resided in urban areas, a 7 percent increase since 1960. The number of cities with populations in excess of 500,000 has increased from two to seven over the past two decades.[1] The growth of Pakistan's major urban centers has been a phenomenon of the postindependence period. Pakistan's largest urban area, Karachi, was a backwater port city of only 360,000 inhabitants in 1947. Today, Karachi's population is approximately seven million. Major urban center growth, although significant, has also been accompanied by a substantial growth of small and medium-sized towns.

Urbanization has been the result of several demographic forces. The first was the settlement of the muhajirin (refugees) who fled India during partition in 1947. Karachi and parts of the Punjab and Sind received millions of refugees. Second, industrial development, which began in the 1950s and increased significantly in the 1960s, stimulated the movement of rural inhabitants to the cities. Third, changes in the rural areas as a result of the spread of agricultural technology in the 1960s contributed to the expansion of the major urban areas as well as the medium-sized towns. Fourth, more recently, the influx of Afghan refugees has increased substantially the population of Peshawar city and division. Finally, returning overseas workers have acquired urban real estate and have resettled in urban areas. Figures are not available to establish the size of this resettlement.

These movements of peoples have changed the physical, economic, social, and political environments of cities and towns in Pakistan. The socioeconomic groups which inhabit Pakistan's urban areas are more diverse than those of even a decade ago. Almost four decades of independence have significantly altered the earlier,

7

predominately rural nature of the country. As this chapter will contend, General Zia ul-Haq's regime is dependent upon these groups for either support or political neutrality in order to maintain power.

Urban Groups

Although Pakistan is considered a South Asian country, this is only partially correct. The people who inhabit its eastern portion (parts of the provinces of the Punjab and Sind) are similar in culture to those found in the Indo-Gangetic plain area in India. Large landlords (zamindars and waderas) tend to dominate these areas. The people of its western and northern portions (Baluchistan and Northwest Frontier provinces) are more akin culturally to those found in the Middle East. Even in urban areas such as Lahore and Karachi, the influx of Pathans and Baluch has altered the South Asian complexion of these cities.

The Upper Class. A highly stratified and authority-oriented urban class structure exists in Pakistan. At the apex of this structure are: (1) the traditional landed elite (many of whom reside in urban areas); (2) the elite civil service; (3) senior officers of the military; (4) industrial-commercial business houses (families); and (5) tribal elites. Except for analytical purposes, these groups are not separate entities. Intergroup marriages have produced family alliances uniting landed wealth with newer industrial-commercial wealth. In other cases, landed wealth has provided the capital necessary to expand into industrial activities. Within the four provinces, the group mix at the apex varies. For example, in the Northwest Frontier province (NWFP), tribal maliks (chiefs) form part of the apex. Although they may own land, their landholdings often are small in comparison to the landholdings of zamindars in Punjab or waderas in the Sind. In Baluchistan, the nawabs (there are four—they are subordinate to the Khan of Kalat; sardars, tribal chiefs, are subordinate to the nawabs) and approximately thirty important sardars (there are over 700) are the most prominent families. Their importance is vested in their roles as leaders of tribal groups. Although during the 1970s the Bhutto government attempted to reduce their political power, their political strength has not diminished substantially even with the settlement of some of their formerly nomadic people.

The greatest change in the urban upper class over the past four decades has been the emergence of the industrial-commercial families. The so-called "twenty-two families" (some analysts maintain there are forty families), chastized by the present Minister of Finance, Mabub ul-Haq, in his famous speech before the

Karachi Chamber of Commerce in 1968, tend to keep a low political profile. However, their economic wealth has provided them with substantial power, and their intermarriage with landed, military, and civil service families has solidified their positions in Pakistani society.

The religious character of these classes is predominately Sunni Muslim although a number of the industrial-commercial families are Shia and Ismailis (a Shia sect). Some of the elite are also Parsis and Ahmadiyyas.

Ethnically, Punjabis, muhajirin, and Pathans dominate the upper classes. The mix of these groups, however, also varies from province to province. Sindhi waderas dominate in upper Sind (outside Karachi), and even with the influx of Punjabis and Pathans into Baluchistan, Baluchi sardars still maintain their strength in the urban areas of that province.

The Middle Class. Perhaps the greatest change in urban class structure in Pakistan over the past four decades has been in the middle class. Increasing affluence, owing to economic development, access to higher education, and overseas worker migration, has permitted upward class mobility. An unskilled overseas worker can earn more than five times the wage rate for the same work in Pakistan. Overseas workers are diligent savers and remit over $3 billion annually. When the worker returns to Pakistan, his savings elevate him several notches financially above his counterparts who did not migrate. In Baluchistan, for example, returning overseas workers have become "mini-zamindars" and shopkeepers. Consequently, over the past decade, these workers have modified the class structure which existed at partition.

For analytical purposes, several groups make up the middle class in urban areas. These include: (1) medium- and small-scale businessmen/shopkeepers, including the so-called "bazaar wallas"; (2) professionals whose families may possess some land but not of the size to provide the only source of financial support for their families, such as doctors, engineers, teachers, intellectuals, college/university professors, lawyers, and technicians; (3) middle class military officers; (4) midlevel civil servants, labelled by some analysts the "bureaucratic middle class"[2]—in the case of Pakistan, for example, those who can progress only up to Grade 17 in the All Pakistan Unified Grade System; and (5) the clerics—ulama, mullahs, and other religious scholars. Given the preponderance of the public sector in Pakistan, groups (2) and (4) are often interrelated. A good portion of the primary and secondary educational system is government operated; hence teachers are part of the public sector. Likewise, universities and colleges are government operated so university personnel are part of the governmental system.

These groups harbor grievances within their class strata and between their strata and the elite, grievances which are often the result of government policies and actions. For example, since the coup in July 1977, the military as a group has benefited from its predominant power position. Military organizations such as the Fauji Foundation (organized as a social welfare institution for retired army personnel) have expanded their operations to include the production of all kinds of commodities and have invested in land. Many Pakistanis maintain that the foundation's prosperity would not have been as great if the military had not been in power. Military officers (retired and active) occupy civil service positions that were previously reserved for civil officers. These activities have not gone unnoticed by other middle class groups, and resentment, at least in private conversations with businessmen, civil servants, and professionals, is expressed. Likewise, hostility is often expressed by the bureaucratic middle class toward the elite civil service because of the former's blocked promotion beyond a certain grade level. Provincial Civil Service (PCS) officers, examples of the bureaucratic middle class, often resent the elite civil service whose officers are trained at the elite Civil Service Academy and enter the civil service at a grade at which most PCS officers retire. Middle class businessmen are critical of government officials (the bureaucratic middle class) with whom they must deal to secure licenses, foreign exchange, and so on. In addition, the more secularly oriented among these groups have disdain for the clerics whom they consider to be illiterate, hidebound transmitters of a backward interpretation of Islam. Finally, resentment exists between the more established middle class groups and those overseas workers who have returned to Pakistan enriched to the extent that financially they are at par or above their former class superiors.

The Lower Class. The urban lower class in Pakistan can also be divided into groups. These include: (1) low-level government workers; (2) industrial workers; (3) the traditional working class (including artisans, manual laborers and servants); (4) petty street vendors; and (5) what S. J. Burki has labeled "urban marginals."[3] The latter group includes those who lack steady employment and literally live on the margin through legal or illegal pursuits.

These groups also have their own hierarchy of status, with government and industrial workers' groups ranking higher than the other three. Groups (1) and (2) have grievances against the government, grievances based primarily on economics. Industrial workers cannot strike, but, at the same time, it is difficult for industrial firms in the private sector to fire them. The urban marginal group has formed the basis for protest against former governments and against the present government. The disturbances in upper Sind during the late summer and fall of 1983 contained elements of this group, and, although the burning of the American Embassy and attacks upon the American consulates general in Lahore and Karachi in 1979 were organized by students, it is suspected that the mobs which participated were composed largely of urban marginals.

Perhaps the greatest changes in the lower class have come from the expansion of the industrial and the government workers' groups. In addition, the overseas migration of industrial workers and members of the traditional working class has changed the nature of both groups and, in some cases, opened up employment opportunities for the other urban lower class groups and for the lower class newly arrived from rural areas. It could be argued that one reason why the lower class has not "taken to the streets" in protest against the present government is a perception that opportunity for upward mobility still exists because of the continuation of overseas worker migration.

Other Urban Groups. Other groups of importance in urban areas cut across class divisions both vertically and horizontally. These include women and college and university students.

The role of women in Pakistani political life has been significant if not thoroughly researched. The pre- independence Pakistan Movement involved elite women in particular.[4] At the basic, family level, and despite the dominant role of men in Islamic society, women contributed to decisions to migrate from India to Pakistan during partition. One of the most famous Pakistani women, Fatima Jinnah, the sister of the Quaid-i-Azam Muhammad Ali Jinnah, challenged Muhammad Ayub Khan in the presidential election of 1965. In more recent times, women were active in the Pakistan People's party (PPP) movement in the 1970s, and the most notable leaders of the PPP today are Nusrat Bhutto and Benazir Bhutto, wife and daughter of the late prime minister, Zulfiqar Ali Bhutto. Women served in the national and provincial assemblies in the 1970s. General Zia appointed women to his cabinets and to the Federal Advisory Council, or majlis-i-shura (in fact, women and minority members of this council staged a walkout in protest of a number of clauses related to the evidence of a woman or a member of a minority community in draft legislation of the Law of qias and divat). Finally, women have been elected as district counselors in the local bodies elections of 1979 and 1983 and stood for election in the national and provincial assemblies in February 1985. Women have also been active in attempts to modify the extremes of Zia's Islamization program. In addition to the walkout from the Federal Advisory Council, women have staged other protests. For example, in 1983 the wife of General Abbasi, then governor of Sind, was part of a women's protest against the antifeminist remarks made by a mullah on Pakistan television. Women barristers have also been arrested and incarcerated for their activities in protest against the present government's policies. However, for the most part, only upper and upper middle class women have been politically active.

Many of today's prominent Pakistani activists first became politically active as students, and student organizations have plagued previous governments. They participated in the protests which led to the downfall of Ayub and campaigned vigorously for Bhutto in 1970. Since 1977, students have been both supporters of Zia and of his political opponents. Student politics in the universities and colleges have pitted those student organizations aligned with the religious Jamaat-i-Islami party against those aligned with the PPP. The issues which motivate students are similar to those motivating their elders: concern for the distribution of economic rewards (jobs and economic opportunities, in particular) and the desire for more involvement in the political process.

Attitudes and Opinions of Urban Groups Regarding the Zia Regime

Before analyzing the attitudes and opinions of urban groups regarding the Zia regime, some general comments regarding issues of concern to Pakistanis provide a basis for this analysis. These issues have their roots in developments which have occurred over the past four decades.

Pakistanis are highly sensitive to economic issues. The so-called "pocketbook" phenomenon noted by American public opinion pollsters has been a factor in national politics in Pakistan since the 1960s. Both the downfall of President Ayub in 1969 and the overwhelming victory of the Awami League in East Pakistan in the 1970 election had strong economic undertones. The strong showing of Bhutto's PPP in the same election in West Pakistan owed, in large part, to his campaigning on the issues of "land, bread, and shelter." It could also be argued that if fair elections had been held in March 1977, Bhutto's majority would have been reduced because of the adverse economic conditions that affected the country.

This brief interjection of political economy is important to understanding why urban classes on a national scale have not been actively involved in antigovernment activity since 1977. Rather, these classes and their counterparts in the rural areas have exhibited political apathy, with the exception of the upper Sind disturbances mentioned earlier and occasional processions in the cities led by bar associations. The economy of Pakistan has been dynamic, and the distribution of economic rewards has not been skewed only to the upper class. Further, as noted above, the overseas migration of close to two million Pakistanis (primarily unskilled workers) to the states of the Persian Gulf has brought a level of prosperity to the lower and middle classes.

But, as some might say, man does not live by bread alone. Among the middle class in particular, there is a desire for more opportunity to participate in a democratically based political system. And even though part of the upper class (the military, elite civil service, and selected civilians) participates in political decision making, the regime's opponents (at the top leadership level) are from the same elite strata.

Since his takeover in 1977, Zia has attempted to provide political participation (referred to as "window-dressing" by his opponents). In 1978, he appointed federal ministers principally from the Jamaat-i-Islami, the principal right-wing religious party. In 1979, Zia announced the "local bodies" scheme whereby each province would organize and hold local elections on a nonpartisan basis for district and union council seats. These elected local officials are responsible for small-scale development projects and have funds for these projects assigned to them. Elections for local councils were again held in 1983. In 1980, Zia appointed new federal ministers and, through his military governors in the provinces, appointed civilian ministers in the Punjab, Sind, and Northwest Frontier provinces. In 1981, Zia established an appointed body at the federal level, the majlis-i-shura, whose only responsibility was to debate public issues, within limits.

In 1984, Zia held a referendum on his performance and his future. Although the government claimed a substantial turnout (over 90 percent), sources close to the Election Commission maintain that only 20 percent of the eligible electorate actually cast their "votes." This event appears to be a source of embarrassment to Zia, even though the press continues to report on groups meeting with him to express their "felicitations" regarding his successful referendum.

Finally, Zia announced that elections to the national and provincial assemblies would be conducted on February 25 and 28, 1985, on a nonpartisan basis. After first restricting candidacy quite severely, he reversed himself and stated that only those convicted by special tribunals would be disqualified. In essence, the elections could have been contested by such vigorous opponents as Benazir and Nusrat Bhutto, as well as by Air Marshal (retd.) Asghar Khan, the leader of the Tehrik-i-Istiqlal party. After a meeting in Lahore in January 1985, the response from the leaders of the opposition's eleven-party Movement for the Restoration of Democracy (MRD) was negative—any members of their parties would be excommunicated if they stood for election. (Another party leader, the Pir of Pagaro who heads the Muslim League, Pagaro faction, responded by stating that his party members were encouraged to run for election since this would give them practice for the real elections!)

The Western press reported a moderate turnout for the February 25 National Assembly election, despite the national boycott called for by the MRD. Before this election, Zia stated that he would be satisfied with a 40 percent turnout. Many rural and working class areas in the cities appear to have exceeded that figure, and random checks at polling stations made by journalists revealed turnouts as low as 20 percent and as high as over 50 percent. The government reported that the turnout was 52 percent of the nation's 36 million eligible voters.[5] Although there were some sporadic incidents of violence, most of the voting was peaceful.

These issues and events form the backdrop for the analysis of group opinions regarding the present regime. The opinions form the basis for conjectures regarding support or the absence thereof for General Zia. As a caveat, the absence of survey research to determine public opinion must be stressed in reviewing the following analysis.

The Upper Class. The traditional landed elite and the industrial- commercial houses have supported Zia and the military junta on most policy issues. To a degree, this support is the result of a fear of the return of "Bhuttoism" and the PPP. Although some landed elite in Sind and the Punjab supported the late prime minister, many zamindars were distrustful of him. Zia has attempted to persuade both groups to collaborate with the regime, and a review of the membership of the majlis-i-shura supports this assertion. Major business houses have been encouraged by the government to invest in and to take over the denationalization of firms nationalized by the Bhutto government. However, these houses have not rushed in to take advantage of government offers. Zia's pledge not to nationalize private sector firms was also made to reassure the business houses of the government's intention to preserve private enterprise. Are these two groups strong supporters of Zia? While they do support Zia, their support cannot be considered especially enthusiastic. Both groups realize that they must be able to work out some kind of modus operandi with whomever holds power. A more systematic analysis of the recent elections would probably reveal landed elite participation but, as has been the case in the past, little participation, at least as candidates, by elders in the industrial–commercial houses.

The senior military officers and the members of the elite civil service have been deeply involved in policy making and administration in the present government. But there are differences in their roles. During the Zia regime, the military has become much more involved in policy making and administration than it was under the previous regimes (Ayub, Yahya and Bhutto). This involvement has diverted a portion of the officer corps from its professional military role. The military's stake in the Zia regime (or a friendly successor) is substantial. On the other hand, with the exception of a few at the very top, the elite civil service has not been as influential under Zia as under Ayub or Yahya. Unlike the military, the elite bureaucracy's support would be more like that of the industrial-commercial houses: prepared to support Zia but not at the cost of sacrificing its position if a new, nonmilitary regime assumed power. The elite civil service suffered under Bhutto, and many officers would not relish a return of the "Bhutto days."

The last group, tribal elites, differs in its attitudes towards Zia. In the NWFP, tribal maliks have tended to support Zia since the Soviet invasion of Afghanistan in 1979. In fact, the movement for an independent Pushtunistan nation has ceased since 1979 (although it was rumored in late January 1985 that several maliks in the Khyber Pass region were "hosting" Soviet agents). As long as the government does not negotiate an adverse (to the Afghan mujahidin) settlement with the Soviets and does not intrude substantially into drug trafficking, important to some maliks, the NWFP will not become a hotbed of antigovernment activity. Baluchistan represents a different situation. Although Zia ended the civil war in Baluchistan when he assumed power in 1977, the major tribal leaders oppose him. Khair Bux Marri resides in Kabul, while it is rumored that Ataullah Mengal and Ghaus Bux Bizenjo have made their peace with Nusrat Bhutto and that Bizenjo has been active in the MRD. The question remains to what extent these three leaders could stimulate confrontation between the Baluchis and the government in Quetta and other cities in Baluchistan.

In summary, Zia still commands support among the bulk of the elite. This support, however, is not enthusiastic among groups outside the military. Even within the military, there has been at least one notable attempted coup (in January 1984), which resulted in the arrest and incarceration of some forty military officers. At social gatherings, where the members of the landholding elite and the industrial-commercial houses are present, it is not unusual to hear critical comments about Zia's policies. Members of the elite civil service are more circumspect, but even they criticize his referendum and his efforts at Islamization. Perhaps Zia's support among these groups results more from an absence of an immediate, preferred successor and from Zia's ability to avoid drastically alienating these groups. In addition, the economy has been dynamic. The Russian occupation of Afghanistan has also provided an immediate, external threat to the country, and has triggered both military and economic assistance from abroad.

The Middle Class. Ayub, Bhutto, and Zia all received support from this class. Ayub assisted middle farmers in their emergence as an agricultural force. Bhutto's success in the 1970s was based on appeals to the middle class and very active support from the professional and student groups of this class. Neither Ayub nor Bhutto had the support of the clerical middle class—a class that Zia, through Islamization, has actively cultivated.

Medium and small-scale businessmen and shopkeepers have so far provided support for the regime. When the bar associations in the Punjab called out processions in support of the disturbances in upper Sind in 1983, their expectation that the bazaar wallas would close down their shops was unfulfilled. Foreign goods are currently more plentiful in the city bazaars than during past regimes. Business appears to be booming. However, this group's support of the regime is not characterized by enthusiasm. At the same time, the opposition parties appear not to have made significant inroads among this group. As long as the economy does not stagnate or decline, this group will support the present regime.

Professionals are less supportive of the Zia regime. Zia's continued martial law and the imposition of both shariah courts and military tribunals, as well as the regime's volations of human rights, strike directly at the legal profession. Lawyers have been most supportive of the MRD. Teachers have staged processions against government policy, primarily to protest adverse pay conditions. The medical profession has been neutral, except in refusing to perform amputations as punishment for theft. Engineers and technicians have been neutral. Journalists continue to pursue their profession, albeit within the framework of a controlled press—a situation not unlike that which prevailed during both the Ayub and Bhutto administrations.

Middle class military officers currently pose no threat to the Zia regime. The continuation of this situation is contingent upon the absence of widespread rioting in the cities and towns in the Punjab. If rioting occurs in the Punjab, and civil authorities (the police) cannot control it, the military units employed to suppress this violence could mutiny. Any such mutinies would probably be led by middle class officers. This has never happened in Pakistan, although the urban violence during both the Ayub and Bhutto periods contributed to changes in national leadership in both cases. What makes the present situation different from the past is that the military is in power. Are members of this group strong supporters of General Zia? This is a difficult question to answer. There was a recent coup attempted against the government, but it is not known which officers participated. Zia himself comes from a middle class family which migrated to Pakistan from the Jullundur district in India, but the extent to which middle class military officers identify with him through shared values is unknown.

Civil servants who are not part of the elite civil service are basically as supportive of Zia as they were of his predecessors. While desiring a bureaucratic system that would offer them more upward mobility, this group does not engage in opposition to authority nor would such opposition alter the system in the fashion they desire. During the Bhutto period, when the government reformed the bureaucracy and opened up senior positions through lateral entry, these officers did not benefit unless they were also active members of the PPP. Despite its lack of opposition, however, this group appears not to provide a vigorous support base for Zia.

With the exception of some Shias, right-wing clerics have identified with Zia's attempts at Islamization. The more traditional among this group support his piety and applaud his introduction of Islamic law. Shia clerics and the Shia community have differed strongly with Zia over his introduction of zakat (mandatory monetary tithe for the poor) and may harbor sympathic feelings towards the Islamic revolution in Iran—a revolution whose leader has condemned Zia. Nontraditional clerics, and there are some, are more closely aligned with Zia's opponents. Clerics were actively involved in the movement which brought down Bhutto. On the other hand, Zia's personal behavior and his reputation as a devout Muslim contrast greatly with those of Bhutto. While disagreeing with him on issues related to the state and Islam, clerics do not pose a threat to Zia's continuation in power at this time.

In summary, with the possible exception of right-wing clerics, middle class support for Zia is similar to that of the upper class. Many feel that the military has been in power too long. The results of the February 25, 1985, election for National Assembly seats reveal both support for and opposition to the regime. Seven of Zia's cabinet members lost, along with thirty other candidates endorsed by him. Certainly some were defeated because of local issues or personal reputation and style, but it may be conjectured that others were defeated because of their involvement with the present regime. Given the reported turnout of 52 percent, the MRD boycott was not highly successful, since its goal was to prevent a turnout of more than 10 percent. The vote itself is an indication of a desire for political participation, a goal of middle class groups in particular. The turnout and the vote against Zia candidates also demonstrate the lack of strong middle class support for the general.

The Lower Class. The most politically active urban lower class group has been the industrial workers. In the protests against the Ayub regime in 1968 and 1969, industrial workers (and sometimes their unions) played a role in the processions brought out against the government. Bhutto was able to capitalize on industrial workers' discontent, and this group supported his campaign in 1970. Industrial workers continued to support him during his tenure in office. However, this group has grievances against the present regime. The labor measures Zia has employed are seen as favoring business. Strikes by workers are prohibited. Unions are stifled. However, given the large temporary worker exodus to the Gulf states, the demand for skilled workers in particular has risen along with wages for skilled labor. Even unskilled industrial labor has benefited—wage rates for unskilled construction workers in cities such as Peshawar have risen from three rupees to twenty rupees per day (from 1969 to 1983). (In 1983, one U.S. dollar was worth approximately twelve Pakistani rupees.) The boom in construction in cities such as Karachi, Lahore, and Peshawar has also increased the demand for both skilled and unskilled labor. Consequently, the economic issue has not been a bone of contention between this group and the government. At the same time, industrial workers cannot be considered supporters of General Zia.

Low-level government workers are politically neutral unless the government does not maintain their wage levels. They are dependent upon government and reluctant to engage in activities that might threaten their retention in government service.

Members of the traditional urban working class also appear to be politically neutral. Perhaps their preoccupation with earning a living limits their capacity to engage in political activities. The rickshaw wallas often express their political preferences by affixing portraits of former leaders of Pakistan within their vehicles. Very few have posters of Zia. Likewise, on privately owned trucks, one sees portraits of Ayub but few of Zia.

Petty street vendors have not actively supported any government except Bhutto's. Zia may be an enigma to them. When one walks down the streets of major cities such as Lahore, one finds these vendors selling posters of prominent past leaders of Pakistan—Jinnah, Ayub, and Bhutto—but few of Zia. Whether this is an indication of how these vendors view politics or the low marketability of Zia posters is open to question.

The urban marginal group is the most volatile of this class. The periodic eruption of mob violence in cities most often involves members of this group, but their motivation is not directly related to political preferences or feelings. They can become the "soldiers" of any politically inspired procession, as the events at U.S. installations in 1979 revealed.

In summary, there does not appear to be any issue or issues that cause urban class groups either strongly to support or to oppose the Zia regime. The turnout in urban working class sections in the National Assembly elections was characterized by the press as "heavy." However, the lack of access to details regarding returns in these sections prevents an analysis of worker support of or opposition to Zia. The limited violence that occurred in this election suggests that even the violence-prone members of the urban marginal group in this class were not highly motivated to disturb the peace. On the other hand, it is possible that the low level of violence was a result of the "preventive detention" measures the government undertook, which included the arrest of hundreds of MRD leaders.

Other Urban Groups. For the most part, women's organizations have not taken positions on public policy. Individual women and ad hoc groups of women (such as the one which picketed the Pakistan television station in Karachi) have expressed dislike of aspects of General Zia's Islamization efforts. Privately, in small social gatherings, women from elite groups tend not to discuss politics, at least in the presence of foreigners. The few who do confine the conversation to the issue of Islamization and the extent to which it further restricts the role of women in Pakistani society. Among elite class women, Zia's Islamization efforts have had mixed reactions at best. But given the absence of research on women in Pakistan, it is difficult to ascertain the depth of attitudes and opinion towards the present government. Most of the information is second hand and anecdotal.

Student organizations have tended to divide on the issue of support of or opposition to the Zia regime, but supporters of the regime have generally been most apparent in recent years. During the late 1970s and early 1980s, the regime favored those organizations which had ties with the Jamaat-i-Islami party. In fact, Punjab University experienced student-faculty confrontations, whereby conservative students challenged what professors taught. Professors, furthermore, were penalized by university officials for such matters as referring to Muhammad Ali Jinnah as Jinnah (instead of the quaid-i-azam—the great leader). In some cases, these charges were brought against faculty by students in their classes. The universities have become politicized to the extent that faculty who were not associated with the right wing have been purged. Other faculty have found the situation in the universities so confining that they have voluntarily resigned their positions. Rival student organizations (those aligned with the Jamaat-i-Islami versus those aligned with the PPP) have at times resorted to violence during their confrontations on the campuses. So far, right-wing student organizations have maintained their control of student politics in the universities, and students have not demonstrated against the government in any significant fashion. It appears that except for the right-wing and left-wing activists, the rest of the students are politically apathetic. They neither strongly support nor oppose the Zia regime.

Conclusions

Despite the absence of survey research on urban group attitudes, it is possible to gauge roughly the extent to which elites, the middle class, and the lower class support General Zia. Zia does not act entirely on his own. The junta, composed of the military service chiefs, the governors of the provinces, the civilian finance minister, and the civilian foreign minister, has acted as the principal policy-making body. Some cabinet members also contribute to the development of policy and play roles in its administration. Senior civil servants working in concert with Ghulam Ishaque Khan (the then finance minister until his selection as a senator in 1985) also contribute to policy making and implementation of policy. It is Zia, however, who is in the public eye and receives the credit or the blame for government policies and operations. When Pakistanis speak of government and government actions, Zia's name is freely used. When political humor is expressed, it is most often Zia and the military who are the butt of the joke. However, despite his apparent unpopularity, Zia has the longest tenure in office, after Ayub, of any Pakistani leader. Pakistanis remark that he has been in office too long, but when asked to explain Zia's long tenure as head of state, their responses are often vague. Luck, cleverness, and the ignorance of the masses are common explanations. But except for the thousands who shuttle in and out of confinement on political charges, the bulk of the population has enjoyed relatively prosperous times during the Zia period.

Under present political ground rules, the national leader in Pakistan does not have to be popular. He does not stand for election (despite Zia's claims regarding the 1984 referendum). Controls on his behavior are exercised by individuals who share most of his values, especially his concern about a return of the PPP. There is no uncontrolled mass media to confront him with his foibles. There are no public opinion surveys to determine his credibility or public confidence ratings. Foreign powers such as the United States, European nations, and the nations of the Muslim world (with the exceptions of Iran and Libya) are only mildly, if ever, critical of his policies or his treatment of political opposition. In his reaction to the February 25, 1985, election, American Ambassador to Pakistan Deane R. Hinton stated: "I think the election was a major step on the road to establishing democratic representative institutions," adding that the arrest of opposition leaders was "one of the unfortunate aspects" of the election.[6]

General Zia ul-Haq's success in retaining power is not based on his personal charisma or popularity. Rather, circumstances have been kind to him. The economy has performed exceedingly well (a 6 percent economic growth rate per annum over the past several years), millions of Pakistani workers continue to earn important foreign exchange in the Gulf states and remit a substantial portion of their earnings, his political opposition has been in disarray, and the Russians are entrenched on the western borders of the country. Through economic and military assistance, he has had the financial support of a number of foreign countries, including the United States, several European countries, and the Gulf states.

To conclude, however, that Zia's retention of power has been entirely the result of fortuitous circumstances is to ignore other facets of the political environment and the events that have occurred in Pakistan over the past decade, and to ignore what Zia represents as the head of state. The urban classes analyzed above may have supported him unenthusiastically but, on the other hand, they have not strenuously opposed him. In many ways, it is these groups which General Zia must continue to cultivate and not alienate. Of these, the middle class in particular is quite important, and some additional observations should be made to sustain this point.

Since the Ayub regime, the urban classes—and particularly the urban middle class—have provided a major support base for Pakistani national leadership. Both Ayub and Bhutto drew heavily on the urban population to maintain their power bases. Both fell from power when the urban population became disenchanted. Changes in the structure of production in Pakistan over the past two decades reflect the importance of its urban areas. In 1960, agriculture accounted for 46 percent of gross domestic product (GDP); in 1982, it accounted for 31 percent. During the same time period, industry and manufacturing rose from 28 percent of the GDP to 42 percent.[7] Urban classes have grown in population as well as influence in the political system. Urban middle class groups have also infiltrated positions in Pakistani society that twenty years ago were the domain of the elite classes. The military, for example, has more officers from the middle class than it did earlier. The same may be said for the civil service. An indication of these changes may be the decline in the use of English and the rise in the use of Urdu. Zia's plans for the increased use of Urdu, although opposed by members of the elite and regionalists (speakers of Pushtu, Baluchi, and Sindhi), have support from some of the middle and the lower classes. Islamization, which has also been opposed by elites and some of the middle class, also has support from the more traditional segments of the middle class and the lower class. Zia's Islamization has not been fully implemented—no limbs have been amputated, for example—which may be interpreted as an indication that only gradual changes in behavior are part of this program's design. If reports of a 52 percent turnout in the February 1985 elections are accurate, it would appear that Zia's efforts to provide limited political participation in the system have appealed to at least a portion of the urban classes.

Will urban groups continue to provide limited support for (or at least not actively oppose) Zia and his military associates in the future? Or will the parties of the MRD succeed in promoting active opposition to the regime among these groups? The continued economic growth of the country will be an important factor in answering these questions. The desire of these groups for a greater share in the political process will also play a role in determining General Zia's future. The opposition's best scenario would include a decline in the economy and an unwillingness on the part of these groups to accept the limited political role for them that Zia has thus far provided.

NOTES

[1] World Development Report, 1984 (New York: Oxford University Press), 260.

[2] James A. Bill and Carl Leiden, Politics in the Middle East (Boston: Little, Brown and Company, 1979), 116–28.

[3] Shahid Javed Burki, Pakistan Under Bhutto, 1971–1977 (London: Macmillan, 1980), 193.

[4] See Jahanara Shahnawaz, Father and Daughter: A Political Biography (Lahore: Nigarishat, 1971).

[5] New York Times, February 27, 1985.

[6] Ibid.

[7] World Development Report, 222.

Rural Groups and the Stability of the Zia Regime

Charles H. Kennedy

General Muhammed Zia ul-Haq assumed power in 1977 with two strikes against him in the rural areas. The first was that he succeeded the dynamic and popular self-styled champion of the rural masses, Zulfiqar Ali Bhutto. Bhutto had been moderately successful in mobilizing the rural masses behind his program of Islamic socialism, which was designed to address the aspirations of the middle and small peasants, the bulk of Pakistan's rural population. The second strike was that Pakistan's rural structure was undergoing rapid and potentially very destabilizing change, including rapid population growth, the social consequences of mechanization and the Green Revolution, and the decline in importance of the traditional rural authority structure. However, seven-and-a-half years later, the rural areas have remained relatively quiet. Only in Sind has there been considerable rural unrest, and there it has never seriously challenged the stability of the Zia regime. This paper attempts to explain such phenomena. It is divided into five sections. The first outlines the demographic determinants of Pakistan's rural areas. The second explores the dominant political structure of the areas and offers a typology of Pakistan's districts. The third section traces the effects of Zia's rural policies since 1977. The fourth centers on the outcomes of such policies by examining the content and possible causes of rural instability in Pakistan. The final section offers a glimpse into likely future developments.

Demographic Determinants of Rural Policy in Pakistan

Critical to any discussion of Pakistan's rural groups are three fundamental, if basic, observations. First, Pakistan is primarily a rural state. Although Pakistan is undergoing rapid urbanization, still, according to the 1981 census, over 71 percent of Pakistan's population lives in towns or villages with fewer than 5,000 inhabitants. Such rural dominance is even greater in the Northwest Frontier Province (NWFP) and Baluchistan (Table 1). Second, agriculture and agriculture-related occupations and industries are the mainstay of Pakistan's rural economy. Over two-thirds of the rural labor force is directly involved in agriculture, while the bulk of the remainder is dependent upon the agricultural sector for employment (Table 2). Third, the rural areas suffer from the disabilities associated with extremely rapid population growth. During the period 1972-1981, Pakistan's rural population grew by 11.7 million, an increase of over 23 percent in nine years, while its labor force increased by 4.3 million. Of course, such rapid growth has played havoc with rural development plans and has placed severe demands on an already none-too-efficient local governmental structure.

Unfortunately, Pakistan's agricultural lands are increasingly unable to absorb such burgeoning growth. Indeed, new land brought to cultivation, primarily as a consequence of expanding irrigation schemes, has been purchased at very high cost. Further, much land is becoming exhausted either due to overcultivation or, more commonly, to salinization. Also, some of the richest agricultural lands in Pakistan have been lost to urban encroachments. One consequence is that Pakistan's farm and cultivated acreage actually registered a net decline during the decade of the 1970s.

Pakistan's rural populace therefore finds itself in a dilemma. On the one hand, population is rising inexorably; on the other, arable farm land has reached its limit of expansion. The options in such a situation are straightforward. Rural Pakistanis must either further subdivide already relatively small landholdings, while attempting simultaneously to increase per acre productivity through mechanization and improved farming techniques; or they must seek employment elsewhere. Both options have been pursued with vigor during the last decade. Evidence for the former is provided by the fact that the number of farms has rapidly proliferated in each of Pakistan's provinces (Table 3), while the corresponding mean size of farm and mean acreage under cultivation has plummeted. Evidence for the latter comes from the relatively even more rapid growth rate of Pakistan's urban areas as well as from the large number of Pakistani unskilled or semiskilled workers in the international labor force.

The trends cited are almost certain to continue, if not accelerate; the problems they engender promise to become correspondingly more severe during the remainder of the twentieth century. If one draws a conservative extrapolation of present trends it can be demonstrated that the rural population will nearly double, the mean farm acreage will be nearly halved, and the number of landless unskilled workers will rise to approximately

TABLE ONE

RURAL POPULATION BY PROVINCE, 1972–1981
(in thousands)

Province	1972	%	1981	%	Change
Punjab[a]	28,585	75.5	34,377	72.2	+5,792
Sind (Excluding Karachi	8,430	59.5 79.9	10,786	56.7 78.9)	+2,356
NWFP	7,193	85.7	9,396	84.9	+2,203
Baluchistan	2,029	83.6	3,655	84.4	+1,626
Pakistan – All	48,715	74.6	60,143	71.4	+11,698

[a]Includes Islamabad.

Source: Calculated from Government of Pakistan, Statistics Division, Pakistan Statistical Yearbook, 1984 (Karachi: Manager of Publications, 1984).

TABLE TWO

STRUCTURE OF RURAL EMPLOYMENT, 1971–1980
(in thousands)

Sector	1971	%	1980	%	Change
Agriculture	9,947	70.6	12,318	67.4	+ 2,435
Manufacturing	1,265	9.0	2,023	11.0	+ 758
Retail Trade	779	5.5	1,273	6.9	+ 494
Services	590	4.2	1,150	6.3	+ 560
Transport, Storage	485	3.4	568	3.1	+ 83
Construction	390	2.8	779	4.2	+ 389
Mining	39	.3	29	.2	− 10
Utilities	23	.2	83	.5	+ 60
Finance/Business	45	.3	48	.3	+ 3
Other		3.7		.2	

Source: Calculated from Pakistan Statistical Yearbook, 1984

TABLE THREE

NUMBER OF FARMS BY PROVINCE, 1972–1980

Province	# of Farms Thousands		Farm Area Millions of Acres		Cultivated Area Millions of Acres		% Cultivated	
	1972	1980	1972	1980	1972	1980	1972	1980
Punjab	2375	2544	31.101	29.897	27.720	26.308	89	88
Sind	748	795	9.497	9.207	8.015	7.818	84	85
NWFP	466	528	4.252	4.099	2.806	2.621	66	64
Baluchistan	173	202	4.347	3.892	2.204	2.455	51	63

Source:

Calculated from Government of Pakistan, Agricultural Census Organization, Pakistan Census of Agriculture, 1972 Vol. II, Provincial Reports (Karachi: MPCPP, 1975); and GOP, Pakistan Census Organization, Pakistan Census of Agriculture, 1980 Vol. II, Provincial Reports (Islamabad: MPCPP, 1984).

one-third of the rural labor force by the year 2000. Given such aprojection, political control of the rural areas, let alone stable development, will become very problematic for any future Pakistani government to achieve.

Political Structure of Rural Areas

Curiously, the greatest controversy in recent rural development literature regarding Pakistan is over whether Pakistan's rural areas should be classified as demonstrating "feudalist" or "capitalist" forms of production.[1] Such debate is partially the consequence of the terminology chosen by would-be reformers of Pakistan's rural structure. The West Pakistan Land Commission Report (1959), which was later embodied in Muhammad Ayub Khan's land reform policy, spoke boldly of eradicating the vestiges of feudalism. Similarly, Bhutto, while downplaying the effectiveness of Ayub's reform, justified his own land reform policies (1972/1977) with almost identical rhetoric.[2] It is also a consequence of political gamesmanship. No one wishes to be called a feudalist or to be perceived as supporting feudalist interests. Therefore, Ayub's apologists characterized their predecessors' policies as hand-in-glove with feudal interests; similar charges were lodged by Bhutto against Ayub, and have been lodged by Zia against Bhutto, and the Movement for the Restoration of Democracy (MRD) against Zia. Finally, the issue of feudalism provokes powerful romantic imagery. As any fan of Punjabi films knows, the unenlightened zamindar (big landlord) is the consummate villain. When he is not forcing his favors on the beautiful and reluctant "girlfriend" of the yeoman modern farmer (inevitably the hero), he is attempting to steal the latter's land through the violent antics of his hired thugs.

Advocates of the feudalist interpretation of Pakistan's rural structure stress the predominance of the zamindar. Disproportion-ate to their numbers, these big landlords control the economic, political and social life of rural communities. This pattern is reinforced by a system of informal ties with external political and administrative elites and with kinship ties to other landlords in neighboring villages and mauzas (revenue units). This structure is maintained by a system of coercive mechanisms ranging from tax collectors to hired thugs, designed to prod the recalcitrant peasant back into the fold.[3] Advocates of the capitalist interpretation downplay the importance of zamindars and predict their eventual replacement by a "rural middle class" consisting of small to medium-sized landholders. The latter group are "economic maximizers," highly motivated to introduce the techniques of modern agriculture: improved seeds and fertilizer and increased mechanization. Because of their numbers, they are also likely to rely to a greater extent than zamindars on institutionalized forms of political representation, and they are likely to support the development of political parties and to agitate for greater democratization of the political process.[4]

I contend that both of these models contain a kernel of truth. It is undoubtedly the case that Pakistan's rural structure contains both "feudalist" and "capitalist" elements. It is also true that Pakistan's rural structure is undergoing rapid transformation which will tend eventually to enhance the importance of the small to medium landholders at the expense of the big landlords. I also contend that this process is neither automatic nor unilinear and, perhaps more important to Pakistan's development and politics, that the pace of such transformation has been unequally distributed throughout Pakistan's districts.

The Traditional Power Structure of Local Governments. The archetypical village in Pakistan is divided into a medley of factions. Usually such factions are drawn along biradari (kinship) lines, but they may also be defined by ethnic, ideological, or class rationales and in many cases stem from longstanding personal rivalries between leaders of different factions. The competition between such factions usually concerns the distribution of scarce resources in the village. For instance, the object of competition may be the division of irrigation water, the allocation of governmental funds, the disposition of title to contested land, and so forth. Such factions are headed by local notables; typically land ownership is the sine qua non of "notability," and all things being equal, the larger the holding the more notable the personage.

The dominant pattern is for a faction leader (a landlord) to form a core of support by calling upon his economic dependents (sharecroppers/tenants) and biradari members. The latter may be faction leaders in their own right. With this core established, the faction leader seeks alliances with other factions or with independents, perhaps small landholders. The cement of such alliances is the prospect of benefits, however defined. This pattern is then replicated at ever wider levels of organization, at the tehsil, district, divisional and provincial levels.

The organization of local government institutions in Pakistan's rural areas has been particularly congenial to this style of power distribution. Regardless of local government programs (panchayats, Basic Democracies, People's Works, Local Councils, etc.) the consequences of their implementation have remained constant. Such institutions have been granted only limited authority; they have been dominated, whether formally or informally, by nonelected bureaucrats; given the realities of the rural power structure, their elected members have been drawn predominantly from the landholding class.

The dominant outcome from the interplay of village/local politics and local government institutions has been the emergence and enhancement of personalized politics. Policies are determined according to the interests of successful faction leaders (at whatever level of government), and only indirectly by ideological or class interests. Since such factions are usually controlled by landlords, it follows that the interests of this group are disproportionately represented in the outcomes of public policy. It is also the case that those who cannot meaningfully influence local politics (the landless and small landholders) are systematically underrepresented in policy outcomes.

The Transformation of the Rural Power Structure. Despite these facts, Pakistan's rural structure is undergoing rapid change in the direction of smaller, more efficient farms. The impetus for this change is partly attributable to the increased pressure on land owing to rapid population growth. But this factor has also dovetailed with two other "planned" factors of Pakistan's rural development: the Green Revolution and land reforms. The former, a strategy of introducing high yield hybrid seeds, insecticides, fertilizers, and other modern agricultural methods, places great reliance on the conversion of the small to medium farmer into a "rural entrepreneur." Part of this process requires that the farmer adopt modern agricultural techniques in an attempt to maximize output per acre. The emphasis, therefore, is on the intensive farming of relatively small plots of land, optimally estimated in the literature at 12.5 cultivated acres. The policy logic of land reforms in Pakistan (1960, 1972, 1977) followed a similar strategy. As R. Herring argues, the bases of Ayub's and Bhutto's land reforms were: (a) that "private property is the legitimate organizing principle for society, particularly because of its implications for individual development and political liberty; (b) radical reform entails serious social costs, particularly with regard to stability; and (c) [therefore] landlordism cannot be directly attacked or abolished, but must be transformed along lines congruent with modern, capitalist notions of efficiency and rationality.[5] The purpose of land reforms in Pakistan was not to effect meaningful redistribution of land to the landless, nor to abolish the large holdings of the zamindars, but rather to direct the traditional inefficient utilization of land into more productive channels.

An examination of Table 4 reveals that Pakistan's rural structure has been transformed in the general direction foreseen by the framers of Bhutto's land reforms. The mean size of farms has declined by 10 percent; the mean cultivated holding by 12 percent

TABLE FOUR

SIZE OF FARMS BY PROVINCE
(in percentages)

Province	Tiny <2.5 acres			Small 2.5-7 acres			Medium 7.5-25 acres			Large 25-150 acres			Very Large >150 acres			X Size/ Farm	Number of Very Large Farms
	#	FA	CA	#	FA	CA	#	FA	CA	#	FA	CA	#	FA	CA		
1980																	
PUNJAB	15	2	2	33	14	14	41	45	47	9	33	32	-	6	5	11.8	7,294
SIND	9	1	1	37	15	16	48	50	53	7	27	24	-	7	4	11.6	2,395
NWFP	37	6	8	39	20	25	20	31	36	5	29	25	-	13	6	7.7	1,481
BALUCHISTAN	17	1	1	23	6	6	42	30	35	16	41	40	1	22	17	19.3	2,867
1972																	
PUNJAB	13	1	1	28	11	12	47	47	49	12	36	34	-	6	4	13.1	7,137
SIND	5	1	1	31	12	13	56	55	61	7	24	20	-	8	5	12.7	2,853
NWFP	33	5	5	37	17	21	23	31	36	6	33	31	-	14	6	9.1	2,147
BALUCHISTAN	14	1	1	22	4	6	41	23	31	21	40	44	2	32	18	25.0	4,026

Key: # = number of farms expressed in percentages by provinces; "FA" = percentage of farm acreage by province;
"CA" = percentage of cultivated acreage by province.

Source: Calculated by author from Pakistan Census of Agriculture, 1980 and Pakistan Census of Agriculture, 1972.

over the course of the 1970s. However, this transformation was only partially at the expense of the "very large" landholders (those holding more than 150 acres), the ostensible target of Bhutto's policies. Rather, as the table indicates, the most significant transfer of land came from the "large" and "medium" farmers (those holding 7.5 to 150 acres) to the "small" and "tiny" landholders (those with fewer than 7.5 acres). Indeed, a look at the number of "very large" landlords before and after Bhutto's reforms supports the thesis that Bhutto's land reforms were only selectively implemented. As Herring suggests, they were used as tools against Bhutto's political foes in the NWFP and Baluchistan.[6]

Regardless of cause, the transformation of Pakistan's rural structure has engendered profound social and political change. Two consequences are particularly important. First, the transformation has increased the number of landless underemployed. The combined effect of reduced landholdings and mechanization of agriculture has increasingly forced sharecroppers and some tenants off the land. That is, the function performed by the latter groups, to farm excess agricultural land, has been narrowed. Not only are farms becoming smaller, but mechanization has also increased the amount of land an owner is able to farm himself. Indeed, the high capital costs of mechanization force the eventual eviction of the relatively inefficient sharecropper and tenant. The options available to those evicted are constrained by lack of education and skills. The dispossessed have swelled the ranks of the urban underemployed and taken unskilled positions in the international labor market. Of course, the potential for social and political unrest by such groups is great, though because of organizational constraints any concerted demonstration of antigovernment sentiments will likely be directed by outside sympathizers, perhaps by the former Pakistan People's party (PPP) or the National Democratic party (NDP).

Second, the transformation of Pakistan's rural structure has the potential to alter significantly the bases of local power. The traditional source of political power in Pakistan's rural areas has been ownership of land, and its dominant class has been made up of large landlords. As the number of small and medium-sized farmers increases, however, there is growing incentive for organization along class or ideological lines. This could spur the development of political parties, particularly parties with a populist program. It must be remembered that the rural mainstays of Bhutto's PPP were the small and medium landholders in the Punjab and Sind.

<u>Toward a Typology of Rural Districts in Pakistan</u>. Pakistan encompasses within its borders four major ethnoregional groups whose histories, economic development, and social structure differ

markedly. Given such diversity, it is little wonder that the pace of rural transformation discussed above has proceeded at different rates within the state. Further, given an array of factors, including climate, availability of water, cropping patterns, and distribution of lands, such vectors of change are not associated exclusively with provincial/ethnoregional demarcations. One cannot speak meaningfully of a typical "Punjabi" or "Baluch" farm. Indeed, one must look at much smaller collectivities, at least as small as the district, to discern patterns of rural development in Pakistan.

Two factors are critical determinants of the rural structure of districts in Pakistan. First is the level of mechanization; second, the relative size of farms. The former is critical because: (a) Mechanization is associated with creating a landless class of dispossessed sharecroppers; (b) increased mechanization is associated with an increase in the adoption of Green Revolution techniques which in turn are associated with a variety of political mobilization factors; and (c) mechanization is an indirect measure of wealth. The size of farm is critical because: (a) of the social and political patterns associated with zamindar-controlled vs. small landholder-controlled farms; and (b) size of farm is an indicator of the relative population pressure on the land. Accordingly, data were gathered on a district basis pertaining to mechanization (percentage of farms/district using tractors) and size of farm (mean cultivated acreage/ district) from the Pakistan Agricultural Census, 1980. The conjunction of these two factors provides a useful conceptual typology of farm districts in Pakistan:

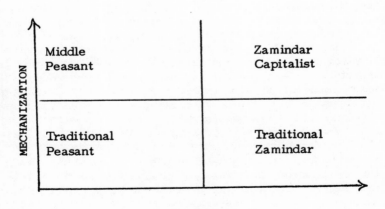

SIZE OF FARM

Traditional zamindar districts were typified by relatively large holdings and low mechanization; zamindar capitalist districts by large holdings and high levels of mechanization; traditional peasant districts by small holdings and low mechanization; and middle peasant districts by small holdings and high levels of mechanization.

The pace of political mobilization and the corresponding potential for rural unrest should be greatest in middle peasant districts for four reasons: (1) Such districts would have a relatively large number of landless former sharecroppers and evicted tenants, potentially very disaffected groups. (2) The traditional faction leaders (landlords) would be greatly outnumbered by middle peasants in such districts. (3) Since landholdings are relatively small in middle peasant districts, it is likely that farmers in such districts would have comparatively greater ties to urban sectors. For instance, second or third sons of small and medium farmers may seek careers in the military or civilian bureaucracy because of the prospect of inadequate agricultural inheritance. (4) The emphasis on education, largely owing to the need for new careers, is likely to be greater in middle peasant districts.

Traditional zamindar and zamindar capitalist districts would be expected to be quiescent by comparison. The traditional patterns of personalized local government and cooptation by federal administrators dovetail neatly with zamindar-dominated systems. Further, the effects of Pakistan's rural transformation would be muted in such districts. Traditional peasant districts would arguably fall somewhere in between. The potential for rural unrest associated with landlessness would be present in such districts, but organizational costs would likely pose a severe impediment to political action. Also, it is likely that such districts would be dominated to a greater extent by landed notables than would be the case in middle peasant districts.

The typology applied to Pakistan's districts is presented in Table 5. It demonstrates that seventeen districts fall in the middle peasant category—ten Punjab districts, four NWFP districts, two Sind districts, and one Baluchistan district. It is noteworthy that in only two of these districts, Nawabshah and Hyderabad, have there been significant rural disturbances since 1977. Perhaps Zia's rural policies help explain this phenomenon.

Zia's Rural Policies, 1977-1985

Zia's regime has not adopted a consciously defined set of integrated rural policies. Rather, the outlines of such a policy have been established largely by default through the adoption of other related sets of policies. Three of these are of particular importance: agricultural policy, Islamization, and the policy

TABLE FIVE

TYPOLOGY OF DISTRICTS IN PAKISTAN

	Small Farms X <11 acres	Large Farms X > 11 acres
HIGH	MIDDLE PEASANT: Peshawar (74); Mardan (73) Lahore (66) Kohat (59); Sialkot (58) Faisalbad; Attock (51) Pishin (50); Gujrat (49) Sheikhbura (43); Sahiwal (42) Nawabshah (40 Jhelum; Kasur; Hyderabad (39) Bahawalpur (38) MWFP Frontier Region (36)	ZAMINDAR CAPITALIST: Gujranwala (59) Vehari (52) Mianwali (48); Quetta (47) Sanghar (46) Multan (37)
LOW	TRADITIONAL PEASANT: Bannu (35) Khairpur; RY Khan; Karachi (34) Muzaffargarh (33) Rawalpindi (32) Loralai (27) Jacobabad (24) Thatta; Shikarpur (23) Swat (21) Cholistan (20) Sukkur (19) Kharan (17) Abbotabad (16) Larkana (15) Turbat (14) Zhob (13) Panjgur (12) Khuzdar (10) Manshera (9) Dadu (7) Dir (5) Lasbela (3) Kohistan; Chitral (0)	TRADITIONAL ZAMINDAR: Sibi (34) Tharparkar (32); Bahawalnagar (31) Sargodha (30); Badin (29) Nasirabad (27) DG Khan (20) Jhang (19) Chagai (18) DI Khan (17) Kalat (9) Gwadur (7) Marri Bugti (4) Kachni (1)

MECHANIZATION (left axis label)

SMALL   LARGE

SIZE OF FARMS

Figures in parentheses refer to percentage of tractor use in relevant districts

Source: Pakistan Census of Agriculture, 1980; table calculated by author

(perhaps "strategy" is a better term) of controlled politics. We will look at the effect of each on rural policy in turn.

Agricultural Policy. Zia's agricultural policy is reminiscent of both Ayub's and Bhutto's approaches. It is assumed that agricultural development will result from a general reliance on the techniques and outcomes of the Green Revolution. Consequently, the Sixth Five Year Plan stresses the importance of "modern inputs" (chemical fertilizers, pesticides, improved seeds) along with the adequate availability of agricultural credit as the keys to growth of the agricultural sector.[7] Also, the plan places great reliance on increased mechanization by proposing a new, locally assembled 20 HP tractor to serve the needs of small to medium farmers.[8] More ambitious is the scheme to increase agriculture acreage in Pakistan by 7 percent during the 1980s by the adoption of extensive and expensive irrigation programs. Indeed, the Sixth Plan calls for increasing expenditures by 100 percent over the Fifth Plan for projects connected with "agriculture and water."[9]

Of course, Zia's reliance on the goals of the Green Revolution has accelerated the process of rural transformation. It has also, perhaps ironically, sown the seeds for the further politicization of Pakistan's rural areas. However, save for the disastrous harvest of 1983-84 in which agricultural production registered a net decline,[10] the performance of the agricultural sector, and by implication Zia's agricultural policies, has been very impressive. The Sixth Plan claimed a net expansion of agricultural product of 4.4 percent per year from 1977 to 1983.[11] Thus, with the potentially destabilizing process of social transformation of the rural areas has come the countervailing trend of increased rural prosperity.

Islamization Policy. Much more widely publicized than Zia's agricultural policy have been his government's attempts to enhance the importance of Islam in the state. Although it is beyond the scope of this paper to explore the Islamization process in detail, it is important to discuss the potential effects of this process on the rural structure of Pakistan.

Potentially of most significance to rural groups is the "pre-emption" legislation currently pending before the federal cabinet for approval. Briefly, such proposed legislation calls into question the validity of government action which restricts the right of property. According to one view embodied in the Council of Islamic Ideology's draft ordinance on pre-emption, Islam does not sanction any state-imposed restriction on land ownership or sale of land, or coercive policies which force the sale or surrender of land by rightful owners. Any such laws, including both Bhutto's and Ayub's land reforms, are therefore repugnant to Islam and must be declared null and void.[12] The Federal Shariah Court, barred from making a binding decision on cases involving such laws, nevertheless argued to the opposite conclusions in the Hafiz Ameen case.[13] The court took the position that although Islam treats private property as sacrosanct, the right of ownership remains subject to the demands of the public good. Therefore, there is nothing repugnant to Islam in the land reforms or any similar legislation.

In the face of such disagreement, Zia's government has moved very cautiously on the issue of pre-emption. This is undoubtedly prudent. First, the stakes of the outcome of such legislation are enormous. Over ten thousand cases challenging one or more laws on Islamic grounds have been registered in the Lahore High Court alone in the past five years. Second, there is considerable sentiment for the adoption of pre-emption legislation in the "landlord-dominated" majlis-i-shura (Federal Advisory Council), a body which has consultative but not legislative powers. Third, the prospective difficulties of implementing an extreme interpretation of pre-emption legislation are staggering. Theoretically, if carried to its logical extreme, title to virtually every piece of land could be made subject to judicial review. However, Zia has delayed action on such legislation until it can be considered by the legislature elected in the national elections of February 25, 1985.

A second outcome of the Islamization process which has had a direct effect on rural groups has been the adoption of ushr and zakat legislation.[14] Ushr is an Islam-inspired land tax assessed at the rate of 5 percent of net agricultural profits beyond a specified minimum. Given the flat rate nature of the tax, and, more important, its likely selective implementation, the effects of the tax are perceived as regressive. Indeed, there have been numerous charges in the press claiming that officials are not enforcing the law, particularly when influential landholders are involved. Zakat, as interpreted in Pakistan, is a wealth tax assessed at 2.5 percent of net financial assets, the proceeds of which are to be distributed to the poor. In practice, however, it has been assessed almost exclusively on bank deposits alone. Since the great bulk of bank deposits are held by urban depositors, it follows that one consequence of the implementation of zakat results in a net transfer from urban to rural areas, ideally to the rural poor. Further, since such transfer is mediated by zakat councils, which predominantly comprise landed rural notables, the notables can claim credit for its dispersal.

A final outcome of the Islamization process has been ideological. Although the adoption of Islamic reforms has been met with considerable opposition in urban areas, particularly by disaffected women's groups, lawyers, and the intelligentsia, it has generated little opposition, if not avid support, in the rural areas. This owes in part to the more traditional outlook of rural society in Pakistan. It is also because of the greater role played by religious functionaries in rural communities. An exception to this generalized image of support is found in some Shia-dominated rural areas. These were alienated by the original compulsory nature of ushr and zakat collection (a violation of Shia jurisprudence). Later, after relevant amendments exempted Shias from participating in the taxes, Shias were alienated by the perception of Sunni cultural domination that allegedly flowed from the Islamic reforms. Compared to urban areas, however, such sectarian-inspired opposition has been mild.

The Policy of Controlled Politics. President Zia assumed power as a consequence of a military coup in 1977. Since that time, his government has pursued a policy of ever greater restrictions on partisan political activity. In 1979, all political parties were banned, and in early 1984, student unions, the last stronghold of partisan activity, were prohibited. Paralleling such political restrictions have been corresponding attempts to legitimize the military regime. Among such attempts have been the Islamization process itself. Other attempts have included the creation of new political institutions and the recent reliance on the holding of partyless national elections.

As early as 1979, Zia's regime established a system of local government with the promulgation of the Local Bodies Ordinances.[15] These ordinances created institutions similar to Ayub's Basic Democracies. Though the ordinances varied from province to province, each established three tiers of local government institutions in rural areas: (union councils, tehsil/taluka councils, and district/zila councils). The composition of the union councils is determined by direct universal suffrage on a nonparty basis; tehsil/taluka councils are composed of union council chairmen, town committee chairmen, and "representatives of nation-building departments" (i.e., bureaucrats); district/zila councils are composed of elected representatives of union councils, tehsil council chairmen, and bureaucrats. Provisions have also been made in each of the ordinances to ensure minority representation in such bodies (women, religious minorities, peasants, tenants, workers), but their selection was to be made indirectly by the members of the relevant council. A further restriction on the political activities of such councils is that candidates are prohibited from contesting seats if they previously held posts in former national or provincial assemblies or were formerly members of political parties. Elections to such councils were held in 1979 and 1983. Though no systematic analysis of the composition of such bodies is available, it is very likely that such institutions have been dominated by the traditional holders of power in rural areas, the landed notables. The absence of political parties, the nature of indirect elections for minorities, and the omnipresence of bureaucratic representation each conduce to this end.[16]

Another partyless political institution, the majlis-i-shura, was established in late 1981. As originally constituted, the majlis was an advisory council, wholly appointed by the president for a four-year term. Representation of the landed elite in this body is considerable. At least 40 percent of its original members classified themselves as zamindars in biographies printed in the press.[17]

Since late 1984, Zia's government has introduced a new wrinkle in the legitimization process: the partyless national election. To a limited extent such an approach has been given sanction by the Islamization process through the vehicle of the Ansari Commission Report, which declared political parties un-Islamic.[18] Accordingly, on December 19, 1984, Zia held a national referendum to answer the question:

> Whether the people of Pakistan endorse the process initiated by General Muhammed Ziaul Haq, the President of Pakistan, to bring the laws of Pakistan in conformity with the injunctions of Islam as laid down in the Holy Quran and Sunnah of the Holy Prophet and for the preservation of the ideology of Pakistan, for the continuation and consolidation of that process and for the smooth and orderly transfer of power to the elected representatives of the people.[19]

The consequence of a "yes" vote to the above would also serve in practical terms to elect General Zia president of Pakistan for a five-year term. The outcome of the referendum as officially reported was very one sided. The government claimed a turnout of 61 percent and a 97.71 percent "yes" vote, that is, that Zia had received a mandate. It is impossible from the results given to glean distinctions in rural/urban support for Zia or for his programs. No breakdown of the vote by district was provided by the government, nor is the answer to the referendum question as drafted an adequate indicator of support for Zia in any case.

Following quickly on the heels of the referendum, Zia announced on January 12, 1985, that February 25 would be the date for the long-delayed nationwide elections to the federal and provincial assemblies. Such elections would be held on a partyless basis. However, in a surprise gesture, the ban on the candidacy of former politicians was relaxed on January 13. Despite such relaxation, however, the Movement for the Restoration of Democracy (MRD) announced a boycott of the polls and very few of the MRD's members filed nomination papers by the deadline for such application.

In conclusion, Zia's rural policies have followed well-worn tracks. His agricultural policy could have been written in 1960, and the Local Bodies Ordinances is similar to the Basic Democracies scheme. The most significant departure has been the Islamization process; and potentially the most "revolutionary" is the prospect of pre-emption legislation. Unlike Bhutto, Zia has kept a tight lid on rural politics, and in general it must be argued that Zia's policies have favored the traditional status quo. However, it must also be stressed that the process of rural transformation, potentially very destabilizing, has accelerated during Zia's regime.

The Track Record: Rural Stability?

So far this analysis has presented a case for the potential of extreme political unrest in Pakistan's rural areas because of rapid social transformation, and has outlined Zia's response to such potential: a conscious policy of depoliticization coupled with a stress on maintenance of status quo elite patterns in the rural areas. This section looks at how successful Zia's policies have been from the perspective of dampening political unrest.

It is a difficult task to assess levels of rural unrest in Pakistan. The press has never been the most reliable source of rural news in Pakistan, owing both to governmental censorship and perhaps more importantly to the urban nature of Pakistan's major dailies. Second, indirect methods of getting such information are fraught with difficulties because of the ideological predispositions of informants and experts. Nevertheless, with some measure of confidence it is possible to discern four major examples of rural unrest which have plagued Pakistan's rural areas within the past eighteen months.

The first and by far the best documented example is the MRD disturbance of fall 1983. This disturbance stemmed from opposition parties' demands that elections be held under the terms of the 1973 Constitution. Interestingly, though the movement was designed to be national in scope, it had its greatest impact on five districts of rural Sind: Larkana, Dadu, Nawabshah, Khairpur, and Hyderabad.[20] Coincidentally, these districts also constitute the core area of support for the defunct PPP, Bhutto's political creation. At the heyday of the disturbances, MRD leaders called for a general strike and gained considerable support, halting virtually all government activities in the most affected districts until the MRD leadership was arrested and the crowds dispersed by the police and army.

A second example are the so-called "hari riots" which have taken place in the last year or so in rural Sind. Haris are Sindhi peasants who are often landless or tenant farmers to wealthier landlords. Here agitation has centered on two issues: one political and reminiscent of the MRD movement; the second, challenging the dominance of the Sindhi landlords. There have been reports of several instances of atrocities committed by three groups: landlords, haris and police.

A third example is the so-called Nawabpur Incident. In this case twenty-three "prominent" landlords of Nawabpur (near Multan) were charged with stripping the wife and two daughters of a troublesome tenant and forcing them to parade through the village. The event became a cause célèbre of the Pakistan women's movement, and the perpetrators were tried before a summary military court. Nine of the landlords were convicted, their lands were confiscated, each received fifteen lashes, each was fined a sum ranging from 50,000 to 500,000 rupees, and all were sentenced to lengthy prison terms.[21] A month later, Zia promulgated a new ordinance (Criminal Law Amendment Ordinance, 1984) which made forcible public stripping of a woman punishable by death.

A fourth example of rural unrest have been the "dacoit disturbances" in rural Sind. Such events are interpreted by the government to involve organized crime and the complicity of landlords. In one instance, the press reported the arrest of seventy Hyderabad landlords on charges or harboring criminals; in another, the so-called Thori Incident (named after a railroad crossing near Hyderabad), three Sind University students, alleged dacoits, were killed by the police.

Three conclusions can be drawn from the foregoing examples: (1) Rural unrest has been confined predominantly to rural Sind. (2) Zia has made prominent examples of landlords who commit excesses or demonstrate opposition to his regime. (3) Rural unrest has not occurred to any significant extent in middle peasant districts. Therefore, Zia has been able to avoid the negative effects of social transformation on political stability. The explanation lies in ethnoregional sentiments and the international labor market.

Sindhi Grievances/Punjabi-Pathan Safety Valves. Since 1977, Sind has been the most disaffected province of Pakistan. The history of Sindhi disaffection is a long one, dating back at least to partition. Its causes include the domination of its peoples by the muhajirin community (Indian refugees), particularly in Karachi and in bureaucratic and business communities; the attempted coerced introduction of Urdu as the national language on the recalcitrant Sindhis in the late 1940s and early 1950s; and the promulgation of the One Unit Plan (the consolidation of West Pakistan into one administrative unit) in 1955. But the greatest single cause of

Sindhi disaffection is linked with the career and demise of the late prime minister, Bhutto. Bhutto was the scion of a very prominent landholding family based in Larkana. During his regime, he encouraged Sindhi sentiments by empathizing, at least rhetorically, with their grievances, and by promising to rectify past injustices. Among the policies undertaken by his government were land reforms, which were interpreted in Sind both as weakening the power of the landlords, and as ending non-Sindhi ownership of agricultural land in Sind. Bhutto also nationalized heavy industry, banks, and insurance, and these actions were perceived in Sind as a challenge to the interest of muhajirin; similarly, his civil and military reforms were perceived as detrimental to non-Sindhi interests. Therefore, with Bhutto's ouster and eventual execution by the Zia regime, a Sindhi martyr was created.

Given this history and list of grievances it is little wonder that rural Sind has proven intractable to Zia's policies. As discussed above, the bulk of antigovernment rural political demonstrations and incidents since 1977 have occurred in rural Sind, and particularly in districts associated with Bhutto and the PPP. In such districts it has proven impossible for Zia and his regime to portray themselves as legitimate rulers. Indeed, Zia is viewed at best as a usurper of power, at worst as a murderer of a Sindhi martyr. There is little chance that such perceptions will change as long as Zia remains in power. When such perceptions are coupled with the political pressures generated by rapid social transformation (our model singles out two districts in Sind, Hyderabad and Nawabshah, as particularly amenable to such pressures), it becomes almost certain that such districts will remain prone to political violence, and will remain particularly unstable in the near-term future.

A discussion of the Punjab and NWFP reveals quite a different picture. Since 1977, there have been very few examples of rural political unrest in these provinces. This is despite the effects one would expect from the rapid social transformation of many of the districts within these provinces. Of the seventeen districts our model singled out as experiencing most rapid change, ten are located in the Punjab and four in NWFP. Further, the districts singled out in our model in the Punjab (Lahore, Faisalabad, Sheikhupura, Jhelum, etc.) were strongholds of PPP support. How can this quiescence be explained?

Three suggestions come to mind. First, there is the Punjabi/military factor. General Zia is a Punjabi military officer. Given the level of regional discord in Pakistan, his "Punjabness" is a powerful factor in projecting a positive image in the province. There is a widely held belief, both within and without the Punjab, that Zia's policies have favored the Punjab or represent Punjabi thinking. This, of course, has negative connotations in the Sind, but it provides a bedrock of favorable predispositions in the Punjab. "Evidence" of Punjabi favoritism includes Zia's Urdu language policy, his Islamization program (a Sunni-Punjabi stratagem?); and his insistence on a strong, Punjabi-dominated central government. Similarly Zia's martial background, his authoritarian approach to politics, and his obvious antipathy to the PPP and to the Bhutto legacy have combined to provide a bedrock of support in NWFP, particularly in those districts which border on the Punjab and which are experiencing rapid social transformation (Kohat, Mardan and Peshawar). This also helps to explain the relative quiescence of Baluchistan.

The second explanation has little to do with Zia's policies or personality. Rather, it is concerned with the international labor market. Since the early 1970s, Pakistani workers have increasingly served to swell the ranks of the foreign labor pool in the Middle East. Pakistan was the source of 1.3 million legally registered foreign workers in 1984. Most are unskilled or semiskilled, and most originally come from rural backgrounds; the great bulk of the latter are victims of the rural transformation process cited above. Over 85 percent of the expatriate workers are Punjabis or Pathans.[22] Therefore, the Middle East labor market has served as a sponge for the Punjabi and Pathan landless, a safety valve for social and political unrest. It has also served as a source to supplement rural incomes. The remittances made by expatriate workers back to Pakistan, primarily to family members in villages, were estimated at $2.85 billion in 1984. Since 1977, the total of such remittances has been approximately $15.5 billion.[23] When placed in the context of Pakistan's economy, such amounts are staggering. In 1984, foreign worker remittances were equivalent to 82 percent of other total export earnings or nearly 10 percent of the gross national product.[24] Since the bulk of these funds has been channeled back into the rural areas of the Punjab and NWFP, particularly to districts with surplus labor (i.e., the middle peasant districts), foreign remittances have also served to make the potentially most unstable districts relatively prosperous.

A final explanation for the relative calm of Punjab and NWFP rural districts has been the military benefits factor. It is undoubtedly the case that President Zia has showered the military, and particularly exservicemen, with numerous benefits since assuming power. Among such benefits are a 10 percent military quota in the civilian bureaucracy and guaranteed admission (mostly for retired officers' children) for admission to universities and professional schools. In addition, Zia has resumed the practice of granting retiring military personnel newly reclaimed agricultural land.[25] Recruits to Pakistan's military, like recruits for the foreign labor market, have traditionally been drawn from districts with surplus labor, that is, the middle peasant districts. Indeed,

Stephen P. Cohen states that 75 percent of the exservicemen hail
from only five of Pakistan's districts, four of which fit our model
of the middle peasant district—Jhelum, Attock, Kohat, and
Mardan.[26] Again, the net effect of such military benefits serves
to increase the relative prosperity of those districts with the
greatest potential for unrest.

In sum, Zia's success in rural areas has been mixed. On the
one hand, there has been considerable unrest in Sind linked in the
main to the legacy of Bhutto and long-simmering Sindhi
grievances. In the Punjab and NWFP, the great potential for rural
unrest has been staved off by the happy coincidence (for Zia) of an
increasing demand for foreign workers and spinoffs from Zia's
concern with servicing the demands of the military.

The Future Stability of Rural Groups in Pakistan

The keys to the future stability of rural groups in Pakistan are
the middle peasant districts, i.e., those undergoing rapid social
transformation including increasing pressure on land and
underemployment. Most such districts are located in the Punjab
and NWFP. So far, Zia has been successful in avoiding serious
unrest in these districts through the fortunate coincidence of a
bullish international labor market and from the byproducts of a
century-old military recruitment pattern.

The prospect for Zia's continued success in avoiding future
unrest is dependent on whether the labor market holds steady.
Most indictors reveal that the need for foreign workers in the
Middle East is declining, and that the heavy demand for such labor
in the late 1970s and early 1980s is not likely to be replicated in
the near future. Any major decline in the demand for foreign
workers will have three unhappy effects on the stability of
Pakistan's rural areas and particularly the stability of the middle
peasant districts. First, rural income can be expected to fall as
remittances dry up. Second, unemployment will rise as the demand
for foreign workers decreases. And third, a new class of
potentially very disaffected individuals, former foreign workers
forced to return to the villages, will be introduced into the rural
environment.

It seems certain that Zia's current mix of rural policies will
not be adequate to meet the unalloyed demands of the middle
peasant districts, if and when they are released. Zia has pursued
policies which have served to maintain the status quo, perhaps a
sound strategy in times of low social unrest, but doubtful once
demands become insistent. Furthermore, as long as Zia remains in
power, it is nearly certain that rural Sind will remain disaffected.
However, it is likely that such disaffection will not be adequately

strong or sufficiently united to force him from power, unless coupled with considerable disaffection from Punjab and Pathan rural areas.

The only obvious long-term solution to Zia's dilemma is the eventual repoliticization of the society. This, however, will prove extraordinarily difficult for Zia to accomplish. First, political elites are not likely to cooperate in such a venture, as the MRD boycott of the February 1985 national elections indicates. Second, Zia has never generated much of a personal following. There is no indication that either of these factors is undergoing any significant change.

Therefore, the most likely future scenario is more of the same. Zia will continue to attempt to mute rural demands by restricting political activity and employing a big stick. If conditions worsen in the rural areas, particularly in the middle peasant districts, repression of rural demands will increase. Whether such a process will result in the ouster of Zia depends on the objective conditions of the middle peasant districts, and the level of organization of opposition groups.

NOTES

1. See for instance Karamat Ali, ed., Pakistan: The Political Ecomomy of Rural Development (Lahore: Vanguard Publications, 1982); Hamza Alvi, "Elite Farmer Strategy and Regional Disparities in Agricultural Development," in Hassan Gardezi and Jamil Rashid, eds., Pakistan; The Roots of Dictatorship (London: Zed Press, 1983); Shahid Javed Burki, "The Development of Pakistan's Agriculture," in R.D. Stevens, H. Alavi, and P. Bertocci eds., Rural Development in Bangaldesh and Pakistan (Honolulu: University of Hawaii Press, 1976); and Ronald J. Herring, Land to the Tiller: The Political Economy of Agrarian Reform in South Asia (New Haven: Yale University Press, 1983).

2. Herring, Land to the Tiller, 94-107.

3. Asaf Hussain, Elite Politics in an Ideological State: The Case of Pakistan (London: Dawson, 1979), 46-8.

4. Burki, "Pakistan's Agriculture."

5. Herring, Land to the Tiller, 93.

6. Ibid., 119.

7. Government of Pakistan Planning Commission, The Sixth Five Year Plan, 1983-1988 (Islamabad: Manager Printing Corporation of Pakistan Press, 1984), 106.

8. Ibid., 124.

9. Ibid., 40.

10. The Muslim in a May 4, 1984, editorial claimed that agricultural production declined by 4.6 percent in 1983-4. The government has claimed a much more modest decline of less than 2 percent.

11. Sixth Five Year Plan, 104.

12. Government of Pakistan, Council for Islamic Ideology, Preemption Order (1980) Pakistan Gazette Extraordinary, (December 13, 1980, 427-41.

13. Hafiz Md. Ameen v. Islamic Republic of Pakistan, PLD 1981 FSC 23.

14. Zakat and Ushr Ordinance 1980, PLD Central Statutes, 97.

15. The texts of the ordinances are found in Syed Abdul Quddus, Local Self Government in Pakistan (Lahore: Vanguard Publications, 1981), 110-402.

16. In general the Local Bodies Program has differed from Basic Democracies in two fundamental regards. First, bureaucrats are less dominant in Local Bodies institutions than they were in Basic Democracies. Second, unlike Ayub, Zia has not converted the local governmental structure into an electoral forum for national elections. See Inayatullah, Basic Democracies District Administration and Development (Peshawar: Pakistan Academy for Rural Development, 1964), and G. Shabbir Cheema, The Performance of Local Councils in Pakistan: Some Policy Implications (UNDP Mission Paper, 1984).

17. Calculated by the author from Pakistan Times, December 28, 1981—January 24, 1982.

18. Government of Pakistan, Cabinet Secretariat, Ansari Commission's Report on Form of Government (Islamabad: MPCPP, 1984).

19. Viewpoint, December 6, 1984, 14.

46

20. See Viewpoint, August 18, – November 17, 1983.

21. Dawn, April 9, 1984.

22. Government of Pakistan, Manpower Division, A Report on Pakistanis Working or Studying in Overseas Countries (Revised Version) (Islamabad: MPCPP, 1984).

23. Calculated from Government of Pakistan, Finance Division, Pakistan Economic Survey, 1983–1984 (Islamabad: MPCPP, 1984), 20–1.

24. Calculated from Ibid., 22–3.

25. Charles H. Kennedy, "Policies of Redistributional Preference in Pakistan." (Paper delivered to American Political Science Convention, Washington, D.C., September, 1984).

26. Stephen P. Cohen, The Pakistan Army (Berkeley: University of California Press, 1984), 45.

Pakistan's Economic Performance in the 1980s: Implications for Political Balance

John Adams

The Scene and the Problem

In the mid-1980s Pakistan is enjoying a period of rapid economic growth. If the pace of this growth continues, the country will attain the threshold of middle-income status by 1988-90, an achievement ranking with the Korean and Taiwanese "miracles" of the 1970s. Yet, few nations are as precariously balanced politically as contemporary Pakistan. Despite its surprising longevity, the Zia government is widely perceived inside and outside Pakistan as transitory; however, the answer to the question, "transitory to what?," is not easily determined. Regional and group tensions within the society remain intense and periodically erupt into unfocused violence or directed antigovernmental agitation, such as that of 1983 in Sind Province. Three less-than-friendly states, two of which, Iran and Afghanistan, are in the throes of war and revolution, ring Pakistan, and all have interests and capacities to intertwine their aims with those of Pakistan's internal regional and economic interest groups.

The obvious question to ask about this juxtaposition in Pakistan of economic prosperity and political uncertainty is the degree to which the two dimensions intersect. There are three logical possibilities.

The first line of argument runs as follows: Rapid growth is grounded in substantial structural changes in the economy. These changes touch many aspects of life. Agriculture is being transformed into a commercial sector, with implications for the relative status, power, and wealth of groups such as landlords, middle-sized commercial farmers, and landless laborers. A more educated population is needed, but the status of women and some minorities may be absolutely or relatively declining because of limited access to schooling. These and many other changes point to the possibility of substantial political and social tension arising from economic change. An arguable proposition is that rapid economic growth and structural change are creating a basis for profound discontent and turmoil.

A second plausible hypothesis is the reverse of the first. Rapid growth in Pakistan is yielding and distributing widespread benefits. Remittances from the Middle East are permitting many lower-income families to move up to the middle-income ranks. Agricultural and industrial growth are providing higher incomes to a wide spectrum of people in both sectors. The "frontline" status of Pakistan draws in considerable aid from the West and the Middle East, easing the foreign exchange balance and providing developmental finance. All in all, this perspective would suggest that rapid growth plays a significant role in dampening sources of political unrest.

A final view is that there is little if any relationship between the many positive economic developments in Pakistan and its political future. The political process may unfold according to a sequence of its own, with the key terms in the equation being leadership, manipulation of ideology and symbols, and political organization and mobilization. Even though elections have finally been held (early in 1985), the political process may move unpredictably, shifting at least some power away from Zia and the army, and they may welcome or at least tolerate this movement. Or, as happened with Zulfiqar Ali Bhutto, political forces could gather momentum beyond control, with problematic consequences for the continuation of the incumbent leadership. External developments on any of Pakistan's three borders could exacerbate these unsettling tendencies, or conversely, might engender a unified national effort to deal with the external foe. In any event, economic factors would be overwhelmed by onrushing domestic and international political dynamics.

Which of these three possible scenarios of economic-political interaction is the most defensible is a question worth pondering. Resolving the problem is crucial to examining the relationship between economic development and the political process in Pakistan in the mid-1980s. When one does so, it becomes obvious that all three scenarios contain accurate elements, but that no one position is complete.

Economic growth confers benefits and rewards on many participants. As long as expectations do not outrace the realities of what is becoming possible with growth, for individuals and the state, growth and its rewards undeniably mute economically based discontent. There are few signs that expectations have been unduly raised, although Pakistanis have become accustomed to high rates of growth and to a good deal of liquid wealth moving around in bazaars, the informal sector, and the underground economy. Remittances, smuggling, and the drug and arms trade with

Afghanistan provide ready funds for various sorts of economic schemes. When these activities are added to more legitimate, rapid income growth in agriculture, industry, and foreign trade, it is plain that many Pakistanis are in positions to feel richer. Perhaps many feel that the economy is yielding more to them than they expected. Only a reversal of growth or the drying up of some of the illegal or marginally legal sources of funds could be a source of discontent.

At the same time, economic growth yields relative and sometimes absolute income losses for some groups. Envy can fuel discontent. Regions or groups that feel left out or left behind can be enlisted in political movements. The problem is, then, not one of deciding whether rapid growth is a stabilizing or destabilizing factor, but of assessing and striking a balance between both lines of causation. It is also important to recognize the validity of the third option: that, at least in the short run, external threats or sudden passions acting in the heat of a domestic political crucible may transcend economic concerns.

A Model of Pakistan's Political Economy

Systematic analysis of the interplay of economic and political developments in Pakistan must begin with the articulation of a model. Such a model must allow economic factors to mute or exacerbate centrifugal political forces. It must recognize that the economic factor may at times play a small role in immediate politics.

Central to a model of Pakistan's political economy is the role of interest groups. An interest-group model is particularly useful in studying Pakistan because of the salience and durability of a relatively small number of elite and mass interests. Figure 1 depicts the relationship of interest groups to economic policies and performance. This model was developed and applied in a study of Pakistan's export policy and performance between 1970 and 1982.[2] The core politicoeconomic process takes economic interest groups as the primary actors. Interest groups shape economic policies and these in turn affect economic performance. Causation is circular: Performance may lead to changes in policy, and since the distribution of the benefits associated with a set of policies and with performance results will vary from time to time across groups, groups are impelled to take political action to change policies, or if need be, regimes.

Complicating factors are that policies are not always implemented as conceived and that policies have unforeseen consequences. Too, the core political economic process is constantly affected by exogenous variables that are unpredictable.

FIGURE 1

POLITICS, POLICY, AND ECONOMIC PERFORMANCE

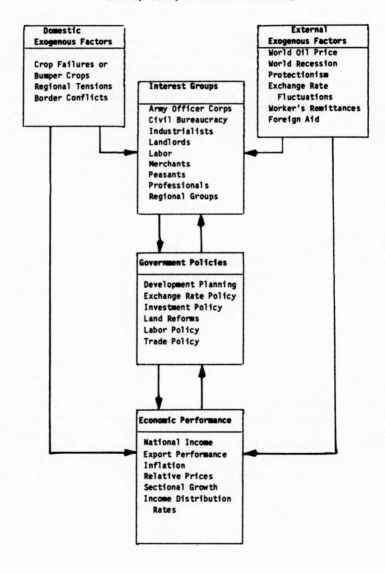

These include domestic factors such as crop failures and external factors such as world recession or the availability of foreign aid. The constant interplay of domestic politics and the random impact of exogenous events mean that the core process is always in a state of flux.

The main economic interest groups in Pakistan since independence have been delineated by Robert LaPorte, Khalid B. Sayeed, and others.[2] As shown in Figure 1, the major elite groups are the military officer corps, the top civil servants, industrialists, and landlords. Each of these small groups controls substantial resources, which differ in kind and are subject to different types of management systems. The principal mass groups are labor, merchants, farmers, landless laborers, students, professionals, and religious sects or clusters. Each of these can be further disaggregated into subcategories (such as big farmers, medium farmers, small farmers; union labor, nonunion labor) or distinguished regionally. No single member of these groups controls significant economic resources or is capable of making a decision that will have effects on more than himself and his immediate family or coworkers. Only in aggregate formations, and in conjunction with each other, can these mass groups have an impact.

Elite groups and mass groups work within the system of political parties, through the media and public meetings, along the vectors of traditional social and family ties, and with other instruments to affect policy.

Interest Groups and the Economy Through 1982

Modern Pakistan has experienced two regime changes. The first was the transition in 1971 from the military rule of Muhammad Ayub Khan to the civil rule of Zulfiqar Ali Bhutto. The second occurred in 1977 when Bhutto was removed from power and Muhammad Zia ul-Haq again instituted military domination. Both developments demonstrate the role of elite and mass economic interests in changing leadership and policy. Mass groups envied the wealth accumulated by a few industrialists under the Ayub government's policies in the late 1960s; many felt they had not shared adequately or at all in the growth process. There was a widespread sense that the economy was not "fair." In addition, policy had strongly favored West Pakistan over East Pakistan. Regional and group concerns over the distribution of the benefits of growth crested in 1970-71 and became one of the bases for mass political movements that split the country and made it impossible for the military to continue to rule.

As head of state, Bhutto undertook substantial economic reforms. His party and government were based on support of the mass groups: urban labor, petty bureaucrats and professionals, small shopkeepers, small farmers, and the landless workers. He attacked the concentrated power of the military officers, industrialists, and chief civil servants through a variety of actions. He attempted to reward his mass followers in urban areas by changing labor's wages and working conditions, a cost to the big industrialists, particularly those in the cotton yarn and textile industry. Bhutto nationalized key industries and greatly shifted the balance of investment from the private sector to the public sector. For his rural supporters, land reform was promised, and there was some attention to agricultural development and input and output prices.

Bhutto found it difficult adequately to reward mass groups because of their sheer size in the face of the government's limited resources and capabilities. Furthermore, the public sector projects were capital intensive and had long gestation periods. They absorbed more resources than they generated in the short to medium run. The economy hesitated under the impact of these dramatic changes, and from 1972 to 1977, weather and external economic conditions put pressure on agriculture and exports.[3] Poor economic performance was a contributing factor in the mounting disaffection with Bhutto's rule and Zia's seizure of power. Bhutto was not able to meet the expectations he had generated in his mass support groups as the economy slowed, and he had difficulty in implementing land reform, helping small farmers, or improving the lot of the lower classes in the towns.

Table 1 summarizes some aggregate measures of economic performance in the three periods just discussed.[4] The Ayub period featured close attention to large-scale industrialization, and this is reflected in the high rate of growth of this sector. Bhutto attacked industrialists—largely the big cotton mill owners—by reducing investment and export concessions, strengthening the position of labor, and letting cotton prices rise relative to yarn and cloth prices, thereby squeezing margins. Agricultural growth was fairly good under Ayub, because his last years brought the initial phases of the Green Revolution, but he was not strongly proagriculture. Although Bhutto tried to do somewhat more for agriculture, bad weather and pest attacks on the crops lowered the growth rate to unacceptable levels. Exports under Ayub grew strongly because of the emphasis on yarn and cloth exports that was part of his industrialization strategy. During Bhutto's time in power, export performance sagged. This is particularly obvious when it is recognized that cotton manufacturers' exports were depressed and that the slack was taken up by a more-or-less

TABLE ONE

STRUCTURAL CHANGE IN PAKISTAN: 1960-1982

(annual average real growth rates)

Year	Agriculture	Manufacturing		Total Exports[a]
		large-scale	small-scale	
Ayub Period 1960-69	3.4	10.9	2.8	9.5
Bhutto Period 1972-77	2.1	3.0	7.3	7.4
Zia Period 1978-82	4.0	9.3	7.3	31.0

[a]Average annual growth rates for the periods 1961-68, 1973-77, and 1978-81.

Source: Government of Pakistan, Finance Division, Pakistan Economic Survey, various issues.

spontaneous expansion of the small-scale manufacturing sectors (leather goods, surgical instruments, carpets).

When Zia came to power in 1977, he appeared to have little capacity to rule or even much interest in staying on for very long. He certainly could not be said to have had a well-conceived economic program or philosophy. In the economic sphere he moved tentatively. His economic pronouncements had much in common with his political pronouncements: They were often vague and contradictory; it was unclear what the timetable would be for implementation; and his policy statements changed with the constituency to which they were addressed. There was a pledge to favor the private sector again, but there was no sharp reversal of Bhutto's nationalizations and no abandonment of large-scale public undertakings. Labor policy was not overturned. A new element was the call for Islamization of the economy. This seemed to amount to no more than changing banking from an interest-paying system to one based on profit sharing. The adoption of the Islamic zakat and ushr tithing and welfare systems was a relatively minor change.

Zia's luck was good on the economic front after 1977. Remittances expanded, and aid continued to flow in, rendering the balance-of-payments gap manageable. The weather was good, and pests were absent. Some serious attention to input prices and input availability created favorable conditions for farmers. Pakistan became self-sufficient in food and has recently exported wheat to Iran. Even a sluggish international economy did not deter Pakistan's exports. Agricultural and small-scale industrial exports rose rapidly.

Pakistan's Current Economic Performance and its Political Significance

The lessons of the transitions from Ayub to Bhutto and from Bhutto to Zia are clear. Leadership in Pakistan cannot stay in power without economic policies that meet the growth and distributional aspirations of a constellation of elite and mass interest groups. Not everyone must be happy all of the time, but very many people must be happy much of the time. Zia and Pakistan's current managers appear to have learned this lesson, and this alone significantly distinguishes them from previous rulers. By luck or design, or out of sensible fear of political reactions to ill-advised economic policy postures, Pakistan's leadership has in place a congeries of economic policies that are working. Perhaps these policies are not so much making the economy work well as simply not confounding spontaneous forces that spring from an innate, cultural Punjabi and Sindhi predisposition to farm aggressively, manage small-scale businesses skillfully, and generally do business in a fashion that brings rewards to individuals and to society at large.

Pakistan's current economic policies fail to meet any test of consistency or coherence. They defy simple labelling. They are capitalist-socialist-Islamic, public-private sector, simultaneously progrowth and prodistribution. By the formal canons of economic planning they appear doomed to fail. External, and some Pakistani, economists are likely to be made nervous by the inchoate policies. Rather than worry, they would be better off trying to understand the nature of Pakistan's unique success in its own terms, rather than contrasting the methods of that success with their own abstract economic philosophies and planning models. That Pakistan is succeeding economically makes a strong if not compelling case for ad hoc planning over ideology, for appeasement over confrontation, for muddling through over rigorous adherence to a systematically derived and esthetically pleasing technical plan frame that delights economists.

In 1982-83, Pakistan's gross domestic product advanced about 6 percent in real terms.[5] Agricultural output was up a strong 4.8 percent, and industrial output rose 8.3 percent. In the previous year, agricultural growth was 3.3 percent and industrial growth was 11.7 percent. In 1982-83, price inflation was between 3 and 5 percent. Exports were up 13 percent, while imports actually declined by 4 percent, easing payments pressures. Remittances were up strongly.

In 1983-84, the Zia government for the first time had to confront some bad economic news. The growth of gross domestic product slumped to 4.5 percent, while agricultural output fell by 4.6 percent. Conditions in agriculture were the worst since 1951-52. The cotton crop was down by about two-fifths because of drought and attacks of pests. Other crops were also affected. Manufacturing growth was still 7.7 percent. Exports appear to have risen by about 15 percent, even with the huge decline in cotton exports. Remittances may have declined slightly.

In 1984-85, early and provisional reports suggested that the economy had returned to the high-growth track. National output is expected to rise by as much as 8 percent, with 9 percent growth in industry and a rebound in agriculture. Exports may be rising at a 15 to 20 percent rate. After a brief uptick during the drought, prices appear once again under control.

The ambitious Sixth Five-Year Plan (1983-84 to 1987-88) got off to a good start,[6] but was scaled down in late 1984. The new plan articulated a tilt toward the private sector, although in view of the mixed philosophical character of Pakistan's operant economic policy, this was perhaps perceivable as mostly cosmetic window dressing to mollify economists from international organizations and foreign aid agencies by saying the fashionable thing. The government is trying to make the existing public sector industries more efficient and is concentrating on infrastructure and the improvement of human resources and the provision of social services. Its projections of high growth rates require substantial mobilization of domestic and external resources for their realization.

The political significance of these post-1982 numbers on the economy is not trivial. The numbers, and the policies associated with them, permit one to make a number of points.

The economy continues to grow handsomely, with a good balance of growth across large and small industry, agriculture, and exports. This growth is apparently conferring its benefits widely across the population. Shahid J. Burki has recently argued that Pakistan is a poor country that, unlike most poor countries of Asia and Africa, has been able to reduce significantly the number of people living in absolute poverty.[7]

The Sixth Plan contained two somewhat contradictory dimensions that demonstrate the ambiguities in Pakistan's economic policy making. There is a strong commitment to reducing controls over and supporting with concessions the private sector so that it will elevate its investment rate and provide much of the growth boost during the term of the plan. At the same time, there is a Bhutto-like commitment to social programs such as education, clean water, and health that represents a socialist dimension in the plan. The government will continue to play a large role in the nationalized industries and is going to expand its role in agriculture. Inputs, technology, and good prices for farm products such as vegetables, fruit, milk, and meat are to be given attention by the government, as rising incomes create large demands. This will supplement previous attention to food crops and commercial crops such as cotton and sugar cane.

The emphasis on the private sector appeases important interests: the country's businessmen, foreign investors, and international agencies and donor countries. All were unhappy with Bhutto's socialism. Liberalization is the chant of the times among world economic policy makers.

The Sixth Plan's stress on basic needs not only sought to pacify, to some extent, internal groups perhaps left out of the game, but it also catered to the more liberal strands of domestic and international opinion. A better-educated and healthier population will be more productive in the long run, so there is an economic payoff. Social programs may act indirectly to bring down Pakistan's high fertility rate, a very desirable consequence. An improved rate of child survival may induce families to have fewer children and concentrate on raising their quality of life.

The way in which the government dealt with the cotton shortfall and its consequences for industrial output, exports, and farmer incomes and security is very significant. The government banned cotton exports and imported cotton. Perhaps $400 million of cotton exports were lost, while $77 million of cotton had to be imported. Fifty-one centers to control pests were established, and farmers were given interest-free loans. The government also acted to deal with rising prices of foods and edible oils associated with the drought.

What these measures mean is that the government took aggressive steps to reduce the negative impact of the cotton crisis on several key interests. The cotton manufacturing sector was helped by provision of cotton stocks. The cotton farmers have been given some relief and help against pests in the future. Perhaps it is wrong to make too much out of this, but it is not clear that earlier governments would have taken the same steps so swiftly and effectively. An economic shock of this magnitude could well have toppled a government that did not or could not react. Earlier governments were operating with more limited resources; rapid growth gives a government, and an economy, the flexibility to deal with intermittent crises. Rapid growth raises government revenues and yields the government resources with which to fight economic brush fires. The perceptiveness, willingness, and ability to deal with such brush fires is a striking development in Zia's Pakistan. Despite his populism, Bhutto alienated many of his supporters within three years of taking power.[8]

To summarize: The rapid growth of the economy after 1977 has undoubtedly played a role in dampening political unrest. Compared to the Ayub era, growth is widespread across sectors and, apparently, across the population. This is not to say that there are not groups which are not participating, or that on a regional basis the effects of growth have been equal. If nothing else, the Bhutto period expanded the role of the public sector in investment, production, and welfare. Zia has not turned away from these dimensions but finds it convenient to create a more favorable environment for private activity. Despite Bhutto's overt socialism, Zia has actually been more successful in appeasing mass groups, in part because he has operated without raising expectations, favorably surprising many by the results his government has obtained. Although his is not a democratic government, it is a government holding precariously to power. Since it cannot rely upon the charisma of its leader or upon strong political roots in mass and elite interests, it must avoid alienating groups by foolish economic measures. The capacity to use growing revenues and power of command over the economy to utilize resources to address troublesome problems, regions, or groups is a key factor that must be watched as this government or a successor struggles to retain power.

Potential Economic Sources of Instability

The roseate picture just painted must not be left unqualified. It is important to examine economic conditions, problems, or tendencies that could create insurmountable problems for Pakistan's leadership.

Economic Ideology. Pakistan cannot afford to pursue extremism in economic doctrine. Pursuit of any pure economic philosophy would surely alienate significant clusters of mass and elite interests. If, for example, the government seriously chased the chimera of economic liberalization and deflected privileges and rewards toward large industrialists and businessmen, many groups would react negatively. Labor is one; high and low bureaucrats entrenched in the system of economic controls are others. Small businessmen might also resent favoritism. Ties between top officers of the army and big businesses, if publicized, would undermine whatever lingering faith there is in the purity of motive of the army's management of the economy.

Liberalization is inconsistent with plans to control the prices and distribution of inputs in agriculture. The price of food matters to both farmers and low-income consumers in the cities. Similarly, prices of edible oils have an impact on family budgets. The price of cotton is important to farmers and to industrialists. The government must not only oversee these prices but it must sometimes create two tiers of prices, one for producers and one for consumers, and fund the difference out of general revenue.

Government management of the economy in Pakistan is implicit in the Sixth Plan and in economic policy statements, even if there is superficial endorsement of liberalization and some moves in that direction. Increased liberalization is not neutral in terms of income distribution and would involve changes as compared with the present situation. Pushing liberalization too far would only make it more difficult for a government to stay in power, because it would mean a warping of incentives and rewards perceivable to many and easily pointed to as a sign of unfairness.

Islamization. Islamization is another ideological dimension with the capacity to push economic policy in directions that would yield discontent. Banking is to be fully Islamized in 1985, with profit sharing replacing the payment of interest, which is banned by the Quran. There is no reason for this to be an unworkable system, although many economists find it strange and unappealing.

The adoption of zakat and ushr is not a major departure and appears as threatening to the normal functions of the economy and government as does the United Way campaign in the United States.

Unless Islamization becomes a stronger force in setting economic policy, there appears little cause for concern. The major problem is that Islamic and non-Islamic minorities feel threatened by a form of Islamization that embodies the doctrines of the majority sect.

Domestic Resource Mobilization. The Sixth Plan required raising the domestic savings rate from its very low 7 to 8 percent to something like 15 percent. (India's rate is over 20 percent.) It is not clear why Pakistan's domestic savings rate is so low, or if it is so low, why the economy is growing so rapidly. One possibility is that the numbers are simply wrong, and that if all of the flows could be properly known, a good deal of capital formation in agriculture and the small-scale sector that is not counted would come to light.

Capital formation has been disappointing in response to the early gestures toward providing support for investment in the private sector. The public sector is still carrying the brunt of investment expenditure. Despite concessions and favorable terms, the private sector has not yet responded to the new liberalization policy with enthusiasm.[9] Perhaps they fear a recurrence of the Bhutto nationalization.

Remittances and Aid. With an acute shortage of domestic capital, Pakistan relies heavily upon remittances and foreign aid. In 1984-85, remittances appear to have peaked. It is unclear whether they will decline or merely stay on a plateau. The plunging price of oil has dried up investment programs in the Persian Gulf states and reduced the demand for migrant labor. If remittances were to fall, and a large number of migrant workers returned, there could be substantial stress on the economy.

Infrastructure and Power. Pakistan badly needs an expansion of its infrastructure. Large and particularly small businessmen have trouble moving inputs and goods around because of delays and inefficiencies. Power shortages are acute, and there is an underlying lack of petroleum and natural gas reserves, although recent discoveries promise to help a little. Rapid growth in industry and agriculture will depend upon double-digit growth of electricity generation and upon at least some new discoveries of hydrocarbons, not only for fuel but as a basis for chemicals and fertilizers.

Refugees and Military Needs. The Afghan refugees in Pakistan are a significant burden on the economy, although external relief helps ease that burden. The longer-term fear is that if the refugees take up residence in Pakistan they will take jobs and land away from local residents. In addition, if the war in Afghanistan reaches into Pakistan with more frequency, military needs could put some strain on the economy. Unlike India, Pakistan lacks much of the industry needed to support its military establishment, making Pakistan dependent upon external suppliers and vulnerable to their manipulation.

Excessive external support for the military, and the commitment of more domestic resources, could put the military in the awkward position of seeming to take more than its share. Under Zia, there has already been a substantial deflection of resources toward the upper echelons of the officer corps and to the military as an establishment. Officers have moved into jobs in business, state enterprises, and government departments. Some have been given access to prime urban land and housing, which they have resold.[10] The use of the military, armed with foreign weapons, against civil disturbances could eliminate the army as a credible political force. It is not even clear that all soldiers and officers would take part in efforts to suppress discontent. Soldiers of one ethnic group would have difficulty firing upon members of their own group; but if, for example, Punjabis were thought to use force easily and excessively in the other provinces, secessionist agencies could mount rapidly.[11]

In sum, military aid and spending are a double-edged sword having as much capacity to destabilize as to stabilize the situation.

Regionalism. Resentment of Punjabi domination is strong in the other regions of Pakistan.[12] Punjab has also had the lion's share of agricultural growth, and its small-scale sector is vigorous. Remittances to the Punjab are strong. Sind has done adequately well, but NWFP and Baluchistan lag behind economically. There are measures in the Sixth Plan to deal with the problem of regional inequality, but they may not be sufficient. At this point regional economic rivalry may be a more important source of discontent than intergroup, ethnoreligious rivalry.[13]

Population and Employment. Pakistan has a very high rate of population growth and very limited success in implementing family-planning measures. Over the long term, the economy will have trouble—and indeed is having trouble—generating jobs. The Sixth Plan attempts to improve the quality of the labor force with attention to education, health, and social programs. The plan strives toward raising the literacy rate from 24 percent to 48 percent. Primary enrollment is to rise 75 percent,and over 81 percent of the villages will have electricity by the end of the plan.

Islamization is to a large degree impeding the education and employment of women. It thereby limits the impact of forces that would lead to desires for smaller families. Over the long run, the questions of the role of women and of population growth must be dealt with effectively.

Conclusion

Recent economic performance in Pakistan, and the policies connected with that performance, have not disenchanted important elite or mass interest groups. This could change if policy became overly ideological and less compromising. The government has been effective in meeting the concerns of many disparate groups, aided by overall growth and expansion of its resources and management capacities. There is a sense that the economy is generating widespread benefits and that the distribution is fair. Regional differences in economic gains are perhaps more important now than intergroup perceptions of inequity.

Economic issues did not seem very important in the elections of 1985. Nor is it likely that the modestly modified distribution of power will yield a much different mixture of economic ideologies or policies. Pakistan will, by the late 1980s, be a rising middle-income country; however, domestic political crisis, attributable to noneconomic factors, could upset this prospect. So could military or other forms of intervention from across the borders, perhaps arising in conjunction with regional secessionism. Disruption of economic growth, and of the pattern of fairly equitable distribution of its benefits across groups and regions, could interact with long-suppressed political discontent to pull Pakistan down into a maelstrom.

NOTES

1. John Adams and Sabiha Iqbal, Exports, Politics, and Economic Development: Pakistan, 1970-1982 (Boulder, Colo: Westview, 1983), 3.

2. Robert LaPorte, Jr., Power and Privilege (Berkeley: University of California Press, 1975), and Khalid B. Sayeed, "Pakistan in 1983: Internal Stresses More Serious than External Problems," Asian Survey 24, no. 2 (February 1984): 219-28.

62

3. Adams and Iqbal, Exports, Politics, and Economic Development, 65-88.

4. Ibid., 233.

5. Marvin G. Weinbaum and Stephen P. Cohen, "Pakistan in 1982: Holding On," Asian Survey 23, no. 2 (February 1983): 123-32.

6. Shahid Javed Burki, "Pakistan's Sixth Plan: Helping the Country Climb Out of Poverty," Asian Survey 24, no. 2 (February 1984): 400-22.

7. Ibid., 414.

8. Lawrence Ziring, "From Islamic Republic to Islamic State," Asian Survey 24, no. 9 (September 1984): 931-46.

9. Sayeed, "Pakistan in 1983," 226.

10. Sayed Serajul Rizvi, "The Paradox of Military Rule in Pakistan," Asian Survey 24, no. 5 (May 1984): 534-55.

11. Stephen P. Cohen, The Pakistan Army, (Berkeley: University of California Press, 1984), 113.

12. Charles H. Kennedy, "Policies of Ethnic Preference in Pakistan," Asian Survey 24, no. 6 (June 1984): 688-703.

13. Sayeed, "Pakistan in 1983," 220-2.

The Military and Security in Pakistan

Rodney W. Jones

Introduction

The security predicament of Pakistan worsened in 1979, when Iranian revolutionary turmoil erupted in the Gulf and Soviet military forces poured into Afghanistan. Pakistan suddenly became a "frontline" state, and the host to thousands of Afghan refugees seeking sanctuary from Soviet repression.[1] The twin specters of Soviet military aggression and political interference thus became direct threats to Pakistan. These were added to Pakistan's longstanding fear of invasion by India. Caught between these two much larger powers—and with its own history of internal instability and vulnerability to dismemberment in 1971 serving as reminders of the "threat from within"—Pakistan's survival as a nation appeared threatened. Predictions that Pakistan would disintegrate became a common journalistic theme.

In context, Pakistan's vulnerability at this juncture seemed greater because of the April 1977 military overthrow of an elected government and the execution of its former prime minister, Zulfiqar Ali Bhutto. For all his political idiosyncracies, Bhutto imparted a sense of pride and momentum to the state after the humiliation of 1971. In contrast, governments of military origin had failed twice before to deal with domestic political change. It was only natural to expect the military intervention of General Zia ul-Haq to be short-lived. If he did not transfer power back to civilians in short order, as originally promised, it seemed likely that the military would be forced out by popular pressure or agitation. Agitation by pent-up political forces might aggravate provincial divisiveness and expose Pakistan to external interference.

So far, these expectations have not materialized. Zia assumed the presidency in 1978 and has, without wholly lifting martial law, survived in power for almost eight years. Moreover, the

63

referendum on Islamization held in December 1984 was designed to provide him a "popular" mandate for another five, further buttressed by national and provincial assembly elections in February 1985. Zia's unexpected longevity has become a factor to be reckoned with. Agitational opposition to military rule thus far has been skillfully diverted or defused. If Zia lasted thirteen years, through 1989, it would be unprecedented for any leader, civilian or military, in Pakistan. Field Marshal Muhammad Ayub Khan's tenure, in comparison, lasted about eleven years.

There is a fair chance that Zia will continue in office, or that the regime he has contrived will last. In view of that possibility, it is worth taking stock of what Pakistan has accomplished on security under Zia and to explore the security problems that Pakistan may encounter downstream. Before doing so, however, it may be useful to note important trends outside Pakistan that shape the context of security perceptions and capabilities, as well as other aspects of international relations in this region.

Regional Security Trends and Context

First, there may be some relief in sight from the most severe pressures on Pakistan stemming from the turmoil in Southwest Asia. The militancy and harshness of the Iranian revolution appear to be moderating, as the institutionalization of the Islamic Republican party government of Ayatallah Khomeini proceeds, and as the adverse effects on Iran of the war with Iraq take their toll. Pakistan is on "cordial" terms with revolutionary Iran, but the repercussions of the Islamic revolution on the Shia communities throughout the Gulf region are a cause of nervousness also in Pakistan; a moderation of fervor naturally puts Pakistan at greater ease.[2]

Shifts in Iranian postrevolutionary politics are reassuring in other ways. It was unclear for some time whether the Khomeini regime would realistically appraise potential Soviet threats in the region, including those resulting from the Soviet invasion of Afghanistan. The displacement of Afghan refugees from the Herat region into Iran was on a much smaller scale than the Pushtun influx into Pakistan; but it was some time before it became clear that Iran had adopted an interest in the fate of Afghanistan. Thus far, it has eschewed direct involvement in negotiations with the Karmal regime or the Soviet Union, but Iran's attitude is no longer so indifferent to the diplomatic bridge-building pioneered by Pakistan and the United Nations.

Soviet perceptions of the cost of an indefinitely protracted conflict in Afghanistan may ultimately be conditioned by active Iranian support for the Afghan resistance, should that materialize.

This would ease Pakistan's burden, at least to the extent it spreads the risk. Other factors could increase the Afghanistan-related pressure on Pakistan; for example, Soviet/Afghan military aircraft intrusions have increased since late 1983. Probably these were intended to counter stepped-up material support for the Afghan insurgents (mujahidin, or warriors for the faith) that flows unofficially through Pakistan. More recently, the new Soviet leader, Mikhail Gorbachev, reportedly gave President Zia a threatening message on the Afghanistan problem when Zia was in Moscow for Konstantin Chernenko's funeral.

The resumption in January 1985 of a U.S.-Soviet dialogue on strategic arms control at Geneva has led some to speculate that the dialogue, by easing East-West tensions, may increase Soviet flexibility on the conditions for their military withdrawal from Afghanistan. Close observers of Soviet behavior doubt, however, that the Soviet Union is inclined to withdraw before it has ensured the objectives that led to intervention in the first instance. However one judges this possibility, the point to bear in mind is that Pakistani expectations may change. Fearing a deal made over their heads, officials in Islamabad may scramble for flexibility and abandon their heretofore principled position on the requirements for a political settlement in Afghanistan.

A third aspect of regional change has been violent political instability elsewhere in South Asia, notably in Sri Lanka since mid-1983, and more recently in India. The growth of political extremism in a splinter group of the Sikh community of Punjab, and the clumsiness of the Indian government's response, bred a confrontation that culminated in the June 1984 army "shoot-out" with extremists at the Golden Temple of Amritsar. This in turn led to the October 1984 assassination of Prime Minister Indira Gandhi and the spasm of sectarian violence against Sikhs in Delhi and other cities. Should serious Hindu-Sikh clashes spread into the Punjab, the Sikh-majority state in India adjoining its namesake in Pakistan, it would further alienate a religious community that has been disproportionately important in India's armed forces, and would represent a potential tinder box for conflagration between the two countries. Moreover, the stability once enjoyed by the Indian subcontinent seems less assured for the future, though it still compares favorably with conditions in the Gulf region west of Pakistan.

Finally, there is in the subcontinent the ominous factor of nuclear proliferation. India demonstrated the capability for nuclear weapons just over a decade ago. Pakistan has been striving since to acquire a similar capability of its own, and there are signs it finally achieved a nuclear weapons capability in 1984. The next few years may see the "weaponization" of Indian and Pakistani capabilities, together with mounting pressures on both countries stemming from a regional nuclear arms race.

The Military in Government

Today, the military leadership of Pakistan dominates government and policy making, and plays the overseer to civil administration as well as the court system throughout the country. Lip service is still paid to the norm of "civilian control" of the military, but practice is just the reverse. Even under civilian governments, the Pakistan military has had a major if not always determining voice in security policy formulation. Today it exercises direct control over all aspects of security policy. During periods of civilian government, the military could advocate its security policy views from a professional perspective. Its increasing assumption of broad public responsibility, however, could mean that its own institutional perspectives on security policy are increasingly influenced by those broader public responsibilities and by various domestic political pressures. Military leaders have become the arbiters of how internal and external aspects of security, and other political, economic and social values of the state, are balanced and integrated. Unfortunately, very little is known about how these issues are articulated or how this balancing process takes place. But since the historical drift in Pakistan seems to be toward the institutionalization of military control over such a process, it is important to understand and to document its implications for Western security interests.

Zia's consolidation of power and longevity probably can be attributed partly to the broadening of military influences in society and the economy, and to the expanding base of civilian participation in the economic infrastructure associated with routine military life, support, and logistics. These may be indicators of the evolution of a distinctive system of governance in Pakistan, a hybrid that merges bureaucratic and parliamentary traditions from the colonial experience with Islamic juridical and representational forms, and that adapts to indigenous social forces embedded in the national mosaic. Indigenous social forces seem to be undergoing an inexorable process of modernization (i.e., participatory expansion and value redefinition), but one that happens to be quite distinct from the Western idiom. In many respects, the future security policy objectives and capabilities of Pakistan may hinge on the outcomes of this process. Major political reactions to military rule, should such occur, may also be shaped by the same underlying process.

Military rule is not "legitimate" in Pakistan, but, as a practical matter, it is widely accepted today. It does not fit the preferred norm, and therefore evokes no enthusiastic public endorsements from articulate sectors of society; it still seems to be an ambivalent matter for most high-ranking military officers. It arouses irritation from politicians and from the professional sectors of society (e.g., lawyers, teachers, and journalists), but it does not provoke broad fury.

Several questions arise: First, what accounts for this underlying acceptance of the military in government? Which sectors of society are most at ease with continued military rule? Are social sectors of dependence on military rule emerging? How much does continued acceptance depend on particular personalities, or on specific methods employed by the government, and how much on economic conditions or other factors that lie beyond full government control? Second, where are the trends leading? What kinds of policy change or fresh development of capabilities are likely to occur that would alter the security environment? How much is subject to planning, and where are the bounds of uncertainty?

Consider the following list of factors as the basis for a tentative explanation of Zia's (or the military regime's) longevity and the spread of significant public acceptance:

1. The internal effects on Pakistan and on Pakistani threat perceptions of the Soviet invasion of Afghanistan.
2. The effects on Pakistani society of expanded income opportunities through migration and reinvestment in a relatively undeveloped economy.
3. The changing social basis of recruitment of the Pakistani armed forces, particularly the army, and the effects on the organization of new entrants with differing values.
4. The expansion of the size of the armed forces and of its domestic infrastructural adjuncts, as generators of employment and opportunities for social mobility.
5. President Zia's (or the regime's collective) cooptational methods and skill in rearranging political constituencies in the nation, of which the Islamization program is but a part.
6. Good luck, which is to say, fortuitous overall economic circumstances and the absence of major warfare.

Repercussions of Soviet Power in Afghanistan

Soviet influence in Aghanistan had little to do with the displacement of the Bhutto government by martial law in April 1977; Bhutto was ousted for internal reasons. But the escalation shortly thereafter of Soviet influence in Afghanistan had profound consequences. Coming in close succession, the Taraki-led Communist coup d'etat in Kabul of April 1978, the violent infighting between the Parchami and Khalqi factions of the People's Democratic party of Afghanistan (PDPA), and the large-scale Soviet military invasion of Afghanistan in December 1979, drastically changed Pakistan's security environment. These events made it far easier for President Zia repeatedly to postpone the promised restoration of civilian rule and faced his regime with major decisions that, in their own way, also added incentives to prolong its tenure.

The arrival of Soviet military power at the frontier of Pakistan crystallized threats that formerly had seemed speculative—and that some still disparage as nothing more than Central Asia's "Great Game." Soviet proximity narrowed the terms of reference or legitimate national security debate in Pakistan, and engendered new constraints, some self-imposed, on those political leaders from Baluchistan and Northwest Frontier Province (NWFP) who stirred "separatist" feelings. Even the sympathy factor for the Bhutto family following Bhutto's execution was inevitably muted by the apparent entanglement of a Bhutto son with an allegedly Kabul-based, KGB-supported terrorist organization, al-Zulfiqar, to which assassination plots against Pakistani political leaders as well as ordinary government employees were attributed.

Close observers of Pakistan usually agree that fair national elections (e.g., as prescribed by the 1973 Constitution) held at any point after the imposition of martial law in 1977 would have returned the Pakistan People's party (PPP) to power, despite the absence of Bhutto, its founding leader. Though loosely knit and undisciplined, the PPP nonetheless retained a widespread popularity in the urban and rural areas of the Punjab, Sind and part of NWFP. This would have given most PPP candidates at least a plurality of votes, and their party, therefore, the majority of seats in the National Assembly.

Once Bhutto had been executed, with Zia's denial of clemency spotlighted by the world, it became improbable that the Zia regime would voluntarily schedule free national elections, unless it could hope to forestall the return of the PPP (as, for example, by a coalescence of other major political parties). The PPP would embody the impulse from Sind, Bhutto's provincial home, to avenge Bhutto's death, and would single out Zia and those of his military associates who were believed to have insisted both that Bhutto be tried for murder, and, if found guilty (under the circumstances then prevailing, a nearly foregone conclusion), that he be hanged without pardon.

The national security sensitivities evoked by the growing Soviet influence in Afghanistan made this unbending treatment of

Bhutto politically sustainable. There was no organized or spontaneous outcry when Bhutto's death was announced; preventive detentions and other actions by the government in anticipation of such a danger were extensive, of course, and on this occasion proved effective.

The lack of compassion by the senior military for their former prime minister's fate probably had roots partly in their concerns about the integrity of the professional military and its role in the external defense of Pakistan. Bhutto's purge of those senior military officers he distrusted (though ironically also the occasion for Zia's sudden promotion over many others more senior than he to the position of chief of the Army Staff) was fiercely resented by a still socially powerful and institutionally loyal generation of professional officers. Perhaps even more important, Bhutto's creation of the paramilitary Federal Security Force—employed as a palace guard, for political intelligence functions, and as a check on the regular military—was seen as a threat to military institutions and a potential political impediment to effective response by the regular armed forces to external threats. The fact that such views may also have been self-serving is beside the point; they would resonate with professional military concerns anywhere. They took on greater importance in the light of increased Soviet influence in Afghanistan. They help to account for the fact that Zia enjoyed continuing support for preserving military control over the government in the early years of his tenure, when his support base was still almost solely the army elite.

The events in Afghanistan also helped Zia obtain support for his interim reconstitution of government with civilian involvement, drawing openly on the conservative religious parties and tacitly on certain centrist political leaders, prior to 1983. Such support played on doubts about the patriotism of the PPP (a "leftist" party, though "social-democratic" rather than "communist"), and led some PPP opponents to suppress their otherwise strong interest in open political competition and termination of military rule.

Migration, Expanded Income, and Social Change

Migration and the inflow of capital from the Middle East—through remittances from migrant workers as well as from more conventional Pakistani exports to that region—seem to be critically important to understanding Pakistan's current political situation. They bear on the longevity of the Zia regime and probably help to account for changing military recruitment patterns and the expanded military involvement—as an interest group—in the economy and politics of Pakistan.

S.J. Burki of the World Bank has tried to estimate the volume
of migration and return flows of capital, and to speculate about the
social and economic effects on Pakistan.[3] He estimates that
Pakistanis resident in the Middle East (even allowing for worker
turnover and returnees) may total between 2 and 2.5 million (more
than twice what official statistics indicate), that the annual level
of remittances from these Pakistani migrants (including informal
channels) is about $4 billion, and that the number of returned
Pakistanis with Middle East experience is about 500,000. Including
workers still abroad, this suggests that some 2.5 to 3 million
members, or about 18 percent, of Pakistan's labor force, has been
involved in external migration. Assuming individual migrant
workers generally represent distinct households, some 25 percent
of Pakistan's twelve million households may have participated.
Since the bulk of the migrants are skilled and unskilled workers,
the participation is disproportionately large in the poorer layers of
Pakistan's population.

This implies broad satisfaction with the present government of
Pakistan, albeit a satisfaction that is neither organized nor vocal
but diffused among a very large number of households in the urban
and rural working classes of Pakistan; it may help to explain the
durability of the regime. It does not represent approval
specifically of a military government nor of Zia personally.
Rather, the military government headed by Zia happens to be the
natural beneficiary of satisfaction with improved material
circumstances.[4]

Social Complexion of Military Recruitment

The effects of the same economic forces on the social
complexion of the military need to be considered. Despite a dearth
of useful data, we may hypothesize that there have been
significant shifts in the attitudes of military officers as younger or
midlevel officers from different social backgrounds move up career
ladders, and, consequently, that there have been changes in the
interest group role of the military. Such hypotheses may shed light
on the degree to which the role of the military in government is
being institutionalized. They may also provide clues to possible
long-term shifts in security policy formation in Pakistan.

Recall that Zia has faced no open political challenge from
within the institutional military. This is not to say there have been
no covert challenges. In fact, there have been reports of several
attempted coups and assassination plots. These appear to have
been mounted by midcareer officer cliques, with perhaps one or
two senior officer patrons. Ideologically speaking, they seem to
have come from opposite extremes, from the radical "left wing" as

well as from Islamic fundamentalists. None of these attempts appears to have had wide reach in the institutional military, however, or to have involved significant numbers of senior military figures, whether serving or retired.

In the past there have also been instances of leftist political radicalism in the Pakistan Army, notably in the Rawalpindi Conspiracy case of 1951; but instances of Islamic fundamentalist militancy within the Pakistani military are new. This may be an indicator of a changing social base and perhaps a different future orientation of the military as a political actor.

Stephen P. Cohen's study of the Pakistan military[5] assembles historical data on the social composition and geographical recruitment pattern of the army, Pakistan's dominant military service. Little seems to have changed about the proportions of recruits drawn from the major provinces, and the primary districts of recruitment still seem to be the same.[6] Yet the social basis of Pakistani military recruitment seems to be changing, not so much along provincial lines as in terms of the social strata that are drawn upon within the dominant recruiting regions.

The commissioned officers of the Pakistan Army who reached retirement age prior to the last decade rose mainly from two social strata. First was that of the major landed families (in the Punjab, NWFP, and, before partition, in north India) representing a gentry or the rural upper class with great social power, and the source also of many prominent political leaders and civil servants. The second was the relatively small urban upper middle class, partly linked by marriage with the rural gentry, and partly upwardly mobile groups that were distinctive to the city. Traditionally, certain males from these families would join the elite civil services, but if they were not quite as good at books, they would elect as a second preference to start officer training in one of the military services.

Today, parents from essentially the same social strata, including senior military officers who themselves used the service to get ahead, frown on military careers for their sons. They prefer rather the prestigious professions, such as medicine, engineering, science, or economics. Their second preferences are to send sons abroad for business administration degrees, enroute, they hope, to jobs in private industry or the public sector. When that does not work out, they may try to set their sons up in a private business, perhaps with the help of the extended family.

As a result, the army has had to dig beyond the traditional elite classes for recruits to officer training, into the middle and lower middle classes of the smaller cities and larger towns. In fact, this shift in recruitment probably began quite some time ago and may have begun before family occupational tastes changed; the postindependence expansion of the armed forces probably required a larger social pool for junior officer recruitment than the traditional notable families could provide. The results have begun to show up recently at the top ranks of the military services, and General Zia actually exemplifies the pattern.

Even more so today, the typical officer recruit is less likely to be from a landed rural or big city background, and more likely to be from a small town. He is less likely to be from a family of notables than from a family that is upwardly mobile by dint of sacrifice and effort. He is more likely to have been reared with values of frugality and discipline, and a stricter and more serious religious outlook. His education may have been in private schools, but seldom in those few elite schools associated with the rich or the landed class, and almost never in elite schools abroad. In general, he is likely to be more conservative in cultural perspective, and less spontaneously receptive to foreign values. In contrast to his predecessors, he will be and seem less westernized or cosmopolitan, but more a natural part of his surroundings. His foreign travel, if any, is more likely to have been confined to neighboring countries or the Middle East. For him, normative concepts such as "civilian control" of the military will have less self-evident appeal and will be subject instead to standards of expediency. He is likely to be gratified by his military career opportunities and, thus, essentially loyal.

One aspect, then, of the stability that Zia enjoys probably results from the changed social composition of the officer class, which increasingly draws on the less cosmopolitan, lower middle classes. Such recruits are more likely to be satisfied with their achievements, compensation, and status in the military, despite the fact that these rewards are now relatively unattractive to earlier generations of senior officers and their families.

Expansion of the Armed Forces

The satisfaction of the military with government, institutionally speaking, may result from better conditions of work and pay, increased fringe benefits, and from promotions that reflect experience and achievement. Better conditions of work would include equipment modernization and support, especially mechanization. External aid and cooperation with Middle East oil-producing states have made it possible for the Pakistan government to provide for such satisfaction, a process that was attended to under Bhutto in notable respects, but expanded further by Zia through greater military participation in the government and administration.

The major expansion in the armed forces of Pakistan came after independence, with the formation of the new state.

Expansion over the last fifteen years has been comparatively gradual; but the input of resources into the military in later years has been substantial. While much of this must have gone into equipment and infrastructure, personnel pay and fringe benefits have also increased significantly. In assessing recent trends, certain watersheds should be kept in mind.

The loss of East Pakistan in 1971 was traumatic for the military; it entailed a humiliating defeat and the incarceration in India of some 90,000 prisoners of war for over a year. It was politically vital for Bhutto's future that the military be cushioned from further distress. Note that by losing the eastern province Pakistan's GNP was about halved, yet essentially the same military establishment (it had been mostly West Pakistani in composition and deployment) was maintained and even expanded. (For supporting data here and below, see Appendix I.) As a result, just to stay even (and not counting the extra cost of the 1971 conflict), expenditures on the military as a proportion of GNP had to double almost overnight. The adjustment was accomplished by about 1974. Pakistan's 1978 (prewar) defense budget was the equivalent of about $605 million; in 1974 it had only reached $713 million, an increase of 18 percent. During the same interval, armed services manpower grew from 324,000 to 392,000 (an increase of 21 percent), largely as a result of the war. In this period, increased resource inputs to the military roughly paralleled personnel expansion.

Modest expansion of the armed forces (mainly the army) followed in two steps: (1) Under Bhutto, in 1976, the armed forces count rose from 392,000 to 428,000 (a little over 9 percent), where it remained almost constant until the Soviet invasion of Afghanistan. (2) Following the Soviet invasion, Pakistan's armed forces climbed by 1982 to 478,000 (an increase of about 12 percent).[7] Meanwhile, the defense budget between 1974 and 1976 rose from the equivalent of $713 million to $1,278 million (nearly 80 percent), running far ahead of the modest personnel growth of the preinvasion period. Some of this could be attributed to equipment modernization; but since there was precious little of that, we can surmise that military personnel benefits were expanding. Some of the growth reflects transfer to Pakistan of a small portion of the new oil wealth in the Middle East. After the Soviet invasion of Afghanistan, defense expenditures rose by 1981 to a level of $1,857 million (about 56 percent over the preinvasion level).

While these macroanalytical figures may conceal as much as they reveal, they indicate that expenditures on the armed forces rose 168 percent (in dollar equivalents) between 1974 and 1981, while personnel expansion in that period increased by only 22 percent. During those years Pakistan procured relatively small amounts of arms from high-cost suppliers such as France, and therefore did not invest heavily in reequipment. Some of the increased investment, therefore, almost certainly went into satisfying the material wants of personnel.

An additional factor contributing to institutional military satisfaction with the government may be the growing numbers of Pakistani servicemen employed by Middle East states under special contractual arrangements. By 1983, there were approximately 20,000 Pakistani military personnel (undertaking guard or internal security duties) stationed in Saudi Arabia alone. These personnel represent almost 5 percent of the Pakistan Army; if they are rotated every two or three years, and if they are paid far more than they would receive in similar service in Pakistan, it suggests not only that a significant fraction of the Pakistani rank and file enjoys special rewards, but that they are getting foreign exposure in a Middle Eastern setting. Moreover, through rotation, the fraction of regular servicemen enjoying such rewards and exposure probably is increasing. It seems likely that Pakistan has been able by such means—the Zia regime being the principal beneficiary—to expand the armed forces but, more important, to increase servicemen's material benefits with only part of the added cost being borne directly by the exchequer (or taxpayer) in Pakistan.

The direct manpower expansion of the armed forces was not particularly impressive under either Bhutto or Zia; the net expansion related both to the 1971 war and the period thereafter was roughly 50 percent. During the same period, Pakistan's population also increased by roughly half, and the male work force probably by somewhat more. Military employment was not used, therefore, to deal with unemployment. If anything did that, it was migration due to overseas earning opportunities in the Midde East and elsewhere.

What may have been more important, however, given added general investment in the military, was the expansion of employment in those ancillary parts of the economy that support the armed services, such as, for example, domestic service, provision of food, construction, and the like.

Looked at this way, the army bulks large in the society and economy, particularly when political parties and other political institutions have weakened or disintegrated. The regular armed forces probably represent nearly half a million households, or about 4 percent of all Pakistani households involved in active employment. If one adds households involved in ancillary services to the military, perhaps another 5 percent would be involved—nearly 10 percent of the households in the nation. Since military recruitment is disproportionately higher in the Punjab and the NWFP, the proportion of households involved directly or indirectly with the military economy would be somewhat higher in those provinces, which are also the main seats of political power. Viewed as a deliverer or producer of livelihoods, the army provides for quite a large share of the population where it counts most. Additional investment in construction of military facilities or in the welfare of the regular military personnel enhances satisfaction in a wide support base. Migratory opportunities in the Middle East probably increase the turnover among those who provide ancillary services to the military, and thus diffuse this satisfaction more widely in society than meets the eye.

The Military In Administration

Under Zia, the senior military (and a small proportion of the rank and file) have become much more deeply involved in government and administration than they ever were before. Given the rewards involved, the military penetration of civil society has become sufficiently pervasive that it is likely to be given up only under duress. The Pakistan military always had a vested interest in political power sufficient to protect its institutional role, its primacy in defense policy making, and its professionalism; today, however, elements of the military also have vested interests in administration in a pluralistic form, and for much more mundane and even personal reasons. Even today, paradoxical though it may seem, the military involvement in Pakistan's government and politics is probably less that of the "institutional military"—that is, the service organizations—than of military leaders who are in transit to second careers.

During his regime, from 1955 to 1969, Ayub deliberately limited military involvement in direct administration of the country, even under martial law; moreover, in 1962 he removed martial law in favor of elected, civilian government. Under Ayub, the senior civil services retained primacy as the senior partner in the civil-military coalition government that prevailed during martial law. During this period, retired senior military officers benefited from the distribution of evacuee property, a few ambassadorships, and some industrial influence-peddling, but there was no major military penetration of administration or new sectors in the economy. The Yahya interregnum (1969-1971) might have been different if it had lasted, but was too short to establish novel precedents.

Under Zia, however, there has been a more extensive military penetration of the administration and industrial public sector, as well as of certain paraeconomic sectors. In the Zia system, the senior civil services seem to be a junior partner to the military, not in numbers, but in the making of policy decisions and in administrative initiative. At the federal level, senior military officers now occupy a large share, perhaps as much as one-fourth, of the thirty-five to forty top bureaucratic posts (i.e., the positions of "permanent secretaries"), which prior to Zia represented a civil service domain nearly impenetrable by serving military officers. Beneath the permanent secretaries, the proportion of military officers in ordinarily civilian posts is smaller, but still substantial; in the past, by contrast, it was nearly zero.

Just as General Zia remains chief of army staff and chief martial law administrator even while he serves as president, senior military officers preside at the provincial government level in dual capacities as martial law administrators and governors, with direct control over the local civil administration. Partially civilian, appointed cabinets also exist at both the federal and provincial levels. At the provincial level, military officers are also intermixed with civilians in high administrative posts beneath the cabinet, and are detailed down to the divisional and even district levels (though in a less conspicuous fashion) to ride herd on civil servants or handle law-and-order problems. Since 1980, there has been a tendency to separate most military officers holding government posts from the direct chain of command. The military governors, for example, were formerly also commanders of army corps commands with direct operational responsibilities. Usually they have remained in government office, while their commands have been transferred to newly promoted officers.

There had been some expectation that Zia would undo the nationalization of industry and banking that Bhutto had promoted; in fact, very few concerns have been returned to private ownership, and none of larger corporations. Instead, this sector has provided the Zia regime with a large pool of well-paid jobs into which he could shift retiring military officers. In this he expanded on a practice, however, that Bhutto had set the precedents for. There are also other aspects of military penetration of the economy. Well known and of long standing is the army's Fauji Foundation which invested in hospitals, industries, and service facilities; today it is a large economic conglomerate in which many retired military officers are employed. A more recent development is the National Logistics Cell (NLC), a trans-Pakistan trucking enterprise connecting Karachi port with the interior. The NLC was created in 1976 under Bhutto to clear emergency grain shipments from overseas that were clogged up in the port. But it now functions as a military-run transportation company, competing with private truckers and with the railroads. For those who know how Pakistan is connected laterally by trunk roads, the potential strategic significance of the NLC is readily appreciated. Reputedly, the NLC is also a channel for illicit traffic and smuggling, particularly of drugs; if so, it could be a less conventional source of material gain that helps to explain the satisfaction within the Zia regime.

The Politics of Cooptation

Much of what has been discussed above relates either to the fortuitous economic benefits to Pakistan of indirect participation in Middle East oil wealth since 1973, or to the distributive functions of a large military organization in a growing economy and changing society—a society where geographical migration and upward income mobility significantly increase the perceived range of opportunities for new earnings or new careers. In a fragmented polity, the military delivers what political parties have been unable to provide for almost a decade; and a very substantial part of today's work force has been employed only since the military came to power. This is no guarantee of continued stability for the regime; it is, however, a substantial part of the explanation for public acceptance.

It is also important, however, to note the degree to which the Zia regime has been sophisticated in its use of instruments of repression, and at least clever in drawing on organized and not-so-organized political constituencies whose former share in power was quite limited. The Zia regime is not without its repressive aspects, but coercion is graduated, usually more psychological or economic than physically injurious when directed against persons. Apart from cases of major riots, which are forcefully suppressed, it only rarely involves death or mysterious disappearances, and is almost invariably "purposive" (in that it fits in with what "government" is expected to do) rather than arbitrary. Zia seems to have been able to avoid personalized or vindictive punitive measures. Cumulative, pent-up alienation, therefore, is not as widespread as it might otherwise be. Only in Sind are there islands of severe alienation today; and there they are by no means trivial.

The other side of the Zia regime is the political cooptation of conservative Islamic interest groups, through favoritism that is politically strategic. The Zia regime's embrace of Islamic legal change goes beyond tokenism; it gives the Islamic political parties (notably, the Jamaat-i-Islami) direct influence in government they have not had before. Their influence has nationalist as well as moral symbolism, and appeals to a growing, indigenous middle class of shopkeepers, small merchants, and new and struggling professionals, who care deeply about the day-to-day progress of their careers or businesses, their immediate families, their neighborhoods, and perhaps their towns and cities. The moral appeal of the Zia regime has been very powerful in these constituencies.

Security Dilemmas: Politics and Security

From the start, Pakistan has been a "security deficit" state. It has severe, indeed, potentially insurmountable, defense problems in the conventional sense of military defense of territory and borders against external threats. In addition, it has deep sources of political insecurity that compound problems of defense against objective military threats. The political threats perceived in Islamabad are not merely to the stability of constitutional government; instability may weaken defense capacity yet need not threaten the survival of the state. Rather, the perceived threats are to the integrity of the state from internal, potentially secessionist political sources (Pashto-speaking tribes in NWFP, Baluchi- and Brahui-speaking tribes in Baluchistan, and Sindhi-speakers in Sind). Probably most objective observers would agree that no internal secessionist force alone has the potential today to break up the country; in this respect, the "nation" of Pakistan is now quite durable. Secession from within could succeed only with deliberate, extensive and sustained help from a neighboring power. Only the Soviet Union or India could each exercise such power and have the needed motivation. From Islamabad's perspective, the possibility that either or both of these powers could and might mount such a threat is a central security policy premise.

Five years ago, one could have said with some confidence that the Soviet Union had not mounted a major subversive effort to inspire secessionist feelings within Pakistan; today the evidence is not so clear. It takes time for clandestine preparation and for guerrilla activities to make headway against an established state. This threat naturally is a part of Zia's calculations; it must also be present in the calculations of Pakistan's external security partners. It is an important basic question, however, whether the current Pakistani regime by its nature or by its internal policies reduces Pakistan's susceptibility to such a threat more or less than would alternative regimes or policies.

The military defense equation between India and Pakistan, as two neighboring countries, is inseparable from the state of their political relations and, indeed, from political conditions within either country as perceived by the other from across the border. Neither country has an incentive and neither is militarily prepared to wage a long war (a "fight to the finish") against the other (though in such an event India's overall indigenous defense production and war-making capacity would clearly be sufficient to overwhelm Pakistan militarily). But both have reasons emanating from the diverse makeup and former interconnections of their societies, as well as their inherently permeable borders, to fear political interference and pressure from the other as an aggravant of internal political troubles. Both have leaned on each other before. Pakistan took political and military initiatives, and India responded or retaliated, over Kashmir in 1965. India used force of arms in 1971 to sever east Bengal. Today, with the Kashmir dispute still unsettled, Pakistan also fears possible Indian initiatives to incite discord or accentuate secessionism in Sind, and India, for obvious reasons, fears Pakistani support for extremist or secessionist Sikh elements in Indian Punjab.

Although the expectation of prolonged war is not high on either side, the capacity to defend successfully against short wars, where one or the other side can occupy territory and use it to bargain for political objectives, becomes imperative. Here the stakes, however, are asymmetrical today. It is barely possible that an Indian military defeat by Pakistan could politically discredit officeholders in India, but it could not plausibly threaten the survival of the country. A defeat of Pakistan by Indian arms however, not only could cause the fall of a government but might undermine the allegiance of dissident provinces, especially if there were a concerted effort to do so.

Unfortunately, Indo-Pakistani security preoccupation with each other diverts both countries from the dialogue and tacit cooperation needed to cope with the threat the Soviet Union poses to the region. Nuclear proliferation and related threats complicate and, unless arrested, probably will further intensify the Indo-Pakistani political and military rivalry.

Afghanistan and the Spectrum of Soviet Threats

Putative Soviet threats to Pakistan are both political and military, with somewhat different near-term and long-term implications. They may be conditioned by the success or failure of the current Soviet strategy for consolidating a dependent regime in Afghanistan, and by the responses of both India and Pakistan, to each other as well as to the situation in the north. They may also be influenced by states outside the region, particularly by the nearby Islamic countries, and by China and the United States.

In the near term, the principal political threats posed by the Soviet Union to Pakistan are of two kinds: One is to the credibility and standing of the current government in Pakistan in the eyes of its own people. The other is to the governability of Pakistan, not so much because of the current regime's standing but because of externally instigated internal disorder that any Pakistani government could find uncontrollable.

The objectives of both types of threats would include: (1) intimidating Pakistan's authorities in hopes they will cut off the flow of support to the mujahidin (though cutting off this flow entirely is almost certainly beyond Islamabad's power); (2) forcing Islamabad to compromise on the terms of an Afghanistan settlement; (3) reducing the level of Pakistan's cooperation with outside powers, particularly China and the United States; and (4) setting in motion trends—though these might not be entirely predictable—that favor the replacement of the current government with one more amenable to Soviet positions. The bottom line would be to make Pakistan more pliable on foreign affairs in the near term, with the end-point being the "Finlandization" of Pakistan.

None of these objectives implies any need for major Soviet military commitments such as would be needed to invade Pakistan deeply. A deep invasion is a remote contingency for various reasons, including logistical ones, as long as the insurgency in Afghanistan remains capable of harassing Soviet military outposts and disrupting overland lines of supply. But the Soviet Union could easily mount with its present Afghanistan-based forces minor ground and major air incursions, using the pretext of "hot pursuit," to damage Pakistani installations or engage small Pakistani military units across the borders—to give the Pakistani military a conspicuous "bloody nose." If this were conspicuous enough to the public in Pakistan, but also clearly not the harbinger of a major invasion of Pakistan, it could discredit the current regime.

This would not work, of course, if the Pakistani military were sufficiently well equipped and prepared to respond, and were lucky enough to inflict a visible "black eye" on Soviet forces in return. But it is doubtful that such a Pakistani response is possible, and it is not even clear that an effort to respond in this fashion is contemplated. The Soviet aim of discrediting the Pakistani regime also might not work if Soviet attacks caused the West to expand substantially military and economic assistance to Pakistan. In fact, to the extent larger Soviet "reprisals" are deterred—as they probably have been—it is almost certainly because of the likelihood they would trigger deeper Western involvement in the defense of Pakistan and much greater support to the Afghan insurgents.

The alternative potential Soviet objective of making Pakistan ungovernable at the grassroots would exploit internal regional and enthnolinguistic differences, but probably not as "nationalist" causes. If the Soviet Union adopted an approach actively supporting the disintegration of Pakistan along subnational lines, it almost certainly would be a long-term rather than a short-term strategy, and not necessarily a preferred one. It is true that the

Soviet Union has exploited subnational groups when expedient (Azerbaijanis, Armenians, Turkomen), but more often when these groups overlap with the Soviet Union than when they do not. More often, the Soviets support the unification, even the regimentation, of heterogeneous peoples (e.g., Vietnamese unification and subjugation of Laos and Kampuchea; the unity of India) and it is clear that they have made no concerted effort thus far to promote Baluchistan or Sind as new nations.

The more likely form of subversion would be akin to what the Soviet Union has done with Afghanistan and with some other regional states (e.g., South Yemen, Ethiopia), which is to promote middle class, intellectual, bureaucratic, and professional military interest in Marxism, together with dependence on the Soviet Union for education, training, technical assistance, and arms transfer. The Soviet approach in Afghanistan was to cultivate urban counterelites and to support them when they seized power. Pakistan is much bigger, and its working and middle classes are more complex; hence the same general approach might not be so feasible. Yet the absolute number of leftist leaders and organizations that could be receptive to such an approach in Pakistan also is larger. The one area that so far seems immune in Pakistan, in contrast to Afghanistan, is the organized military.

The degree to which provincial tension might be a source of ungovernability, with or without Soviet (or Indian) involvement also depends partly on internal migration. Although much more needs to be done to clarify trends, migration within Pakistan probably is changing the face of the country and the corresponding political arithmetic of the provinces. Migration will also stir up local ethnolinquistic friction that will seem disorderly and a threat to political stability. But the longer-term effect may well be to stitch the country more closely together, especially if Pakistan is lucky enough to enjoy freedom from war.

The major trends include Punjabi and Pathan migration to other provinces: Pathans through the transportation-related industries, and Punjabis through the opening up by development or by patronage of a wide range of jobs in more distant parts of the country. An effect of partition and the influx of Muslim refugees from north India in 1947 was that the urban areas of Sind became heavily settled (Karachi overwhelmingly so) by non-Sindhi-speakers. By 1961, Sindhi-speakers represented less than 60 percent of the population of their province. Today, Sindhi-speakers appear to have become, marginally, a minority in their own province, and are much more self-conscious of non-Sindhi (especially Punjabi) encroachment even in the rural areas. The MRD-orqanized demonstrations and the spread of Sindhudesh (Sind "independence") agitation in the province in August-September 1983, reflected Sindhi embitterment at the encroachment of "outsiders" in provincial public employment and on cultivable lands reallocated by the federal government. But the incremental increase of non-Sindhis in Sind's economic and political life is unlikely to be reversed.

A similar process of outsider migration into Baluchistan seems to be fundamentally altering the balance of social power in that province in favor of peoples from other regions, particularly the Punjab and NWFP. Although accounting for nearly 40 percent of Pakistan's land area, Baluchistan twenty years ago contained only about 3 percent of the total population; today the figure is nearly 6 percent. This indicates population movement into the province in proportions that are submerging the original, ethnolinguistically distinct but sparse population.

Pakistan is changing socially and demographically, and the disintegrative "threat from within" is being ameliorated by social change. While it can still be exploited from without, perhaps even more so at present because of the friction migrants generate, eventually it will be less manipulable even from outside. Perceptions of the decline of Pakistan's vulnerabilities, however, may lag behind reality.

Considerable trouble for Pakistan could be generated by Afghan refugees now resident in Pakistan. There is little doubt that the Soviet Union seeks to establish intelligence networks among the refugees to counter the insurgents, and reasonable to assume that pro-Soviet infiltrators could also stir up conflict between refugees and native inhabitants—one more form of working to produce ungovernability within Pakistan. Conflicts over land and water for grazing animals have already occurred, though the degree to which trouble has been averted thus far has been remarkable. The influx of Pushtuns into Baluchistan, where a Pushtun minority existed before, probably will threaten to unseat Baluch-Brahui dominance from another direction.

There is considerable latent concern in Pakistan that the refugees, the longer they are forced to stay in Pakistan, represent a political explosion in the making. However, this is by no means a foregone conclusion, since refugees in most host countries usually subscribe to local order and assimilate into the economy where possible with a generally productive result.

U.S. Security Assistance To Pakistan

U.S. security assistance to Pakistan resumed in 1983, when a $3.2 billion package over six years—roughly divided between economic and military support—finally cleared Congress. While the package helps to support a measure of Pakistani military modernization, a large portion of Pakistan's military acquisitions

will be purchased without subsidy or on the basis of
nonconcessional loans. The most important military benefit for
Pakistan is favored access to the U.S. arms market, including
special permission to buy forty General Dynamics F-16 Hornet
fighter/interceptors, one of the most advanced military aircraft in
the world. Pakistan is also receiving from the U.S. a few Harpoon
antiship missiles, upgraded M-48 tanks, tank recovery vehicles,
towed and self-propelled field artillery, a few armed helicopters,
and second-hand destroyers. Radar equipment purchased from U.S.
companies is also being used to provide aircraft warning systems on
the western border. A major portion of Pakistani military
purchases appear to be possible as a result of financial aid from
Saudi Arabia, the United Arab Emirates, and other Arab
oil-producing countries.

   The crucial significance of U.S. security assistance to Pakistan
is, however, less military than political, especially as it relates to
the Soviet threats. The equipment transactions spread out over
time as they are, are too small and too slow to modernize
Pakistan's armed forces fully. Although they do improve
Pakistan's self-defense capability against India, they are
insufficient even there to narrow a growing gap in conventional
military capability. They are quite inadequate to make it possible
for Pakistan to stand up effectively to a determined Soviet
military invasion. Their central purpose is to strengthen Pakistan
politically, to provide its leaders reasons for self-confidence in
standing up to Soviet political-military pressure. The security
assistance, but particularly the sale of closely held F-16s, is
designed to send a signal to the Soviet Union that it runs added
risks in interfering with Pakistan's security. The F-16s underline
far better than words the importance the United States attaches to
Pakistan's security.

   Nonetheless, U.S. provision of security assistance to Pakistan
creates three dilemmas, one related to Pakistan authoritarian
politics, another to Indian sensitivities, and a third to U.S. interests
in nuclear nonproliferation.

   There are strong U.S. concerns about political and human
rights that are vocally reflected in Congress, and Pakistan does not
pass these tests well. However stable Pakistan's government under
Zia presently seems, it is difficult to believe that it can remain
stable indefinitely. The case can be made that only a
representative government will strengthen Pakistan nationally for
the long haul, despite any near-term instabilities that democratic
politics might generate.

   Ironically, it is a common perception in Pakistan that Zia's
tenure and success in government depend on the good will of the
Reagan administration; Zia held off on finally scheduling the
December 1984 referendum until after the U.S. presidential

84

election (and until it was clear that India would also go to the polls). Moreover, Zia set the ground rules and the February 1985 dates for "partyless" national and provincial assembly elections only after President Reagan had been comfortably reelected. Although there is a gap between the degree of publicly perceived and real U.S. influence, there is a kernel of truth in Pakistani perceptions that the U.S. president actually could be more persuasive in urging Zia to restore a meaningful measure of representative government. It is just possible the national assembly elected in February will produce leaders who can, over time, assert sufficient power to make government responsible.

Indian sensitivities about U.S. arms transfers to Pakistan are inevitable and difficult to ameliorate. Although under Mrs. Gandhi India formally acknowledged Pakistan's right to procure arms for self-defense, Pakistan's security relationship with the U.S. is difficult for India to accept. The main reason for this is not the arms, though the fact that these can be used against India is a concern; the primary issue, rather, is that Pakistan's bolstered confidence makes it more resistant to compromise with India on India's foreign policy desires and approach to regional security. From an Indian perspective, the removal of military tension with Pakistan requires that Pakistan give up external security partners and accept the resolution of outstanding disputes with India on a bilateral basis. Pakistan's unwillingness to do this is blamed on the United States. Further, the prevailing Indian view is that Soviet encroachment on the subcontinent and Arabian Sea is actually stimulated by U. S. involvement in the region, and that Pakistan may ultimately be a victim of its close relationships with the United States and China.

From a U.S. viewpoint, however, this Indian approach is unrealistic and short sighted, and ignores the vulnerability of the Persian Gulf region. Indian sensitivities offer the U.S. no easy choice but to accept that friction with India is part of the price of bolstering security in the region. This, as a result, requires a large and continuous U.S. expenditure of diplomatic effort with India to compensate. As a practical matter, India's close relationship with the Soviet Union makes Indian views on Afghanistan potentially important in any search for a settlement.

Recently, Pakistan has requested U.S. permission to purchase the Grumman E2C Airborne Early-Warning and Control System (AWACS), to enable the Pakistani Air Force to detect and respond quickly with high-performance aircraft to Soviet/Afghan air intrusions. An unstated rationale for the request may have been to enhance Pakistan's capability for detecting and thwarting an Indian preventive military attack on Pakistan's nuclear facilities. Apparently Indian contingency plans for such an attack came to light in the fall of 1984. (The stimulus for the Indian investigation into espionage in its own bureaucracy was, according to some reports, owing to the leak of such contingency plans to foreign sources.) In retrospect, it seems these disclosures coincided with the Pakistani E2C request.

The last point raises a few of the many aspects of the nuclear proliferation problem.[9] An Indian temptation to try by conventional military means to eliminate Pakistan's sensitive nuclear facilities is not unnatural after the precedent Israel set in 1981, when it attacked an Iraqi nuclear facility. But an Indian act of this kind almost certainly would provoke a more substantial war between India and Pakistan; given the Soviet presence, there might well be other unforeseen consequences for the subcontinent. The Pakistani request for the mini-AWACS aircraft shows also that efforts to acquire nuclear weapons will not reduce conventional arms competition, as some speculate, but will rather intensify it.

It is a very high priority, therefore, that the U.S. and other cooperating countries succeed in arresting nuclear weapons proliferation in Pakistan, difficult though that may seem to be under the circumstances. There are few things more likely than the effects of nuclear proliferation to increase Soviet opportunities for extending its influence in the subcontinent.

It is commonly argued that as long as there is substantial forthcoming U.S. military assistance, Pakistan will not test a nuclear explosive device to prove its capability. Although this is probably true, it is not enough to keep a bomb capability untested forever; it is important to secure Pakistan's commitment to abstain from going that route altogether. No future administration would likely have a stronger hand with Pakistan on this matter than does the Reagan administration today.

The Saudian Arabian Connection

The long-term objectives of the United States in Southwest Asia are much the same as those enunciated in the Eisenhower Doctrine: to provide security assistance that increases the self-defense capacity of local powers to withstand the multifarious internal sources of instability and to be able to resist aggressive Soviet influence. These objectives were more vividly understood once the dependence of the West on regional oil had increased and the producer countries took direct control of that resource in the 1970s, and even more so when Iran went through a revolution that impinged on the stability of the other Gulf countries. The art of the possible makes the pursuit of what the early Reagan administration called a "strategic consensus" in the region elusive and untenable. But the orchestration of a network of security relationships among regional states, linked in various ways with the

U.S. Britain, France and the West in general, has been evolving and is becoming more resilient. Saudi Arabia and Pakistan are today, in different but symbiotic ways, pivotal countries in the Gulf regional network.

Pakistan's advantages are that it is able to provide personnel and manpower for security purposes to states that are much weaker or less fully developed in military experience, infrastructure, and the like. Pakistani pilots and soldiers know how to run and maintain various kinds of foreign military equipment, as well as how to integrate it organizationally. They provide a regional source of expertise that is relatively unobtrusive, at least in contrast to Westerners, and yet, being non-Arab (and non-Persian) not caught up in nor likely to become embroiled in the internal disputes of the local countries. They are a relatively "safe" source of help. But Pakistan is also, by regional standards, a fairly powerful country, one with which a network of good relations could prove useful. The formally nonaligned status of Pakistan helps, of course, to make Arab special relationships with Pakistan immune from local criticism and, therefore, potentially reliable.

It is no surprise, therefore, that the two regional countries best known for support of the flow of weapons to the Afghan mujahidin are major Arab states, Saudi Arabia and Egypt. It is true that both have special relationships with the United States, but neither is subservient. Pakistan's acceptance of the flow of arms to the mujahidin probably has more to do with the wishes of these two countries, and their importance to Pakistan's foreign policy, than with U.S. wishes. It is not something that can be made hostage to U.S. "good behavior", or turned on and off to counter Western nuclear nonproliferation pressure.

The Afghan Insurgency

An interesting development late in 1984 was the role of the U.S. Congress in articulating support for the Afghan mujahidin, support that is noticeably (and remarkably) as strong from liberals as conservatives—despite the usual difficulties of associating publicly with covert actions. It was revealed not only that covert U.S. financial support for the mujahidin has been substantial, but also that it is to be expanded to something on the order of about $200 million or more a year; this, ironically, would be roughly the level of total "security assistance" offered by the Carter administration to Pakistan (and about half the annualized level of the Reagan administration's security assistance to Pakistan). Assuming such assistance can be effectively absorbed, it suggests the mujahidin will be capable of a major escalation in their level of activity against Soviet occupation forces. One must ask whether such an escalation will change the regional situation in the subcontinent.

It is doubtful that the Soviet Union will withdraw its forces from Afghanistan until it has consolidated the Karmal regime or a similar successor. The Soviet strategy has become one of forced depopulation ("migratory genocide") of those rural areas in Afghanistan where a combination of intimidation and offers of local truces do not produce an end to serious conflict. It is unclear how long the mujahidin can withstand a "scorched earth" strategy that eliminates their social cover and sources of reprovisioning internally. It is also important to recognize the pluralism of the mujahidin. Pakistan's main dealings are with a limited part of the spectrum of insurgent groups (mainly Pushtuns and, among them, more with Islamic fundamentalists than moderates); it is by no means clear that these groups are carrying out the most successful offensives against Soviet and Afghan forces. Moreover, the recent disclosures of covert aid include allegations—as yet unconfirmed—that some of the aid is siphoned off before it gets to the mujahidin. If such diversion occurs within Pakistan—perhaps it would be best understood as a form of "indirect aid" to Pakistan.

There is some danger that publicly acknowledged and stepped-up U.S. aid to the insurgents will create an added sense of irritation in the Soviet leadership responsible for the conflict in Afghanistan, and greater risks of cross-border retaliation focused on Pakistan. This in turn probably would draw the United States and Pakistan closer. Depending on how it were handled, it could also strengthen Zia's bases internally; the danger to his regime has been discussed earlier: that it could be militarily humiliated.

The Soviet Union may be reluctant, however, to take actions against Pakistan that could be so easily spotlighted to increase Western security support in this fashion. The main reason for this line of speculation is the revival of strategic arms control talks in a European setting—where Soviet stakes are clearly much higher. If one considers psychological momentum as an important feature of such negotiations, or of East-West relations more generally, the Soviet Union currently needs to repair the damage to its image not only from its actions in Afghanistan, but from the repression in Poland and its unilateral "walkout" from the INF and START talks. In short, Soviet escalation of military activity in Afghanistan would entail considerable risks to its own international agenda.

Relations with India

Indo-Pakistani relations turned sharply down in the second half of 1983. Mrs. Gandhi's undue interest (some Pakistanis would say her "gleeful" interest) in the August 1983 Sindhudesh developments put the otherwise useful bilateral discussions—of a nonaggression pact and adjustments on a whole series of matters from Kashmir to removing trade barriers—back in cold storage. India's subsequent difficulties, externally with Sri Lanka (which actually appealed to Pakistan, among others, for assistance), and internally with Sikh extremism in the Punjab, made it more than usually difficult to resume bilateral momentum.

With Rajiv Gandhi's succession and enormous electoral victory in December 1984—bringing the All-India Congress party back with 80 percent of the parliamentary seats that were contested in the election—it must also be said that there are new opportunities. Rajiv has plainly stated that his foreign policy will not change very markedly from the guidelines established earlier, and one would not expect differently. But he has also spoken of working constructively on the relationship with Pakistan, and one must presume that he intends to do so in a measured fashion.

The most important aspect of these developments in India, however, is that they seem to have reduced the prospect of renewed hostilities with Pakistan in the near term. During 1984, a number of harsh statements were made by Rajiv—including one that forecast a war with Pakistan by December. One would usually ascribe these sorts of things to "election politics" and the fact that Mrs. Gandhi's maneuvers in Assam, Punjab, Andhra Pradesh, Karnataka and Kashmir were producing a lot of internal stress. But it was impossible to overlook the temptation, especially in a rough election campaign, to use external threats as a means of unifying the country, and a military adventure—a controlled one, of course—could very well have been used for that purpose.

Thus, while Rajiv's moves seem to be sound so far, it is possible India will return to a more bellicose posture if he encounters problems in the future. But for the time being, Pakistan may enjoy relief from pressure on that side.

NOTES

1. See Allen K. Jones, "Afghan Refugees: Five Years Later," (Washington, D.C.: American Council for Nationalities Service, U.S. Committee for Refugees, Issue Paper, January 1985).

2. In addition to the Afghan refugee problem, Pakistan also has, though on a much smaller scale, an Iranian refugee problem that has received less attention but is a potential source of bilateral friction. Most Iranian refugees in Pakistan are concentrated in Karachi. Though relatively few register with the local office of the U.S. High Commissioner for Refugees, they may number between 15,000 and 20,000. Some are young males of

middle class origin evading military conscription, but their differences with the regime in Tehran are pronounced.

3. See S.J. Burki, "Pakistanis in Middle East – I," The Muslim, December 19, 1984.

4. Ibid. As Burki puts it, "The migration of millions of Pakistanis to the Middle East has had a very calming effect on the country's economy and society." He also warns that "a sharp reversal in the past trends . . . will have some very disturbing consequences."

5. Stephen P. Cohen, The Pakistan Army (Berkeley, CA; University of California Press, 1984).

6. Ibid., 42–44. Cohen points out that British Indian army recruitment during World War II from the area that became West Pakistan in 1947 drew about 77 percent from the Punjab, 19.5 percent from NWFP, 2.2 percent from Sind, and only 0.06 percent from Baluchistan; the limited data available today suggest little change in these percentages. Within the Punjab and NWFP, certain districts were also heavily favored by tradition. Today, 75 percent of all exservicemen come from only three districts in the Punjab (Rawalpindi, Jhelum, and Campbellpur) and two adjacent districts in NWFP (Khat and Mardan)—an area characterized by heavy population density, inadequately irrigated agricultural conditions, comparative poverty, and clannish kinship groups. These districts contain only 9 percent of the male population of Pakistan.

With regard to the composition of officer recruits, Cohen indicates that a 1979 class of students admitted to the Pakistan Military Academy was about 70 percent Punjabi, 14 percent from NWFP, 9 percent from Sind, 3 percent from Baluchistan, and 1.3 percent from Azad Kashmir. But he adds: "There are no data on the social and class origins of these young officers, on their political preferences, on their ambitions and aspirations, or on their aptitude and competence. Although they constitute one of the elites of the state of Pakistan, virtually no scholar has studied them, in part of course, because the military regards such information as a question of national security."
Even with some degree of provincially broadened recruitment, however, because of the institution of provincial "quotas", the underlying regional social composition seems to be changing very slowly. Punjabis and Pathans migrate in significant numbers to the other provinces, and are eligible in other provinces to be part of the provincial quota.

7. During these years, Pakistan increased the number of its infantry divisions from the prewar level of eleven to sixteen, and added sixteen infantry and special-purpose "independent brigades" (the equivalent of over three divisions plus special air defense units) and six armored reconnaissance regiments. See recent issues of The Military Balance London: International Institute of Military Studies, annual series.

8. For a succinct description of military policy in Pakistan and of the role of planned U.S. military assistance in the period after the invasion of Afghanistan, see Shirin Tahir-Kheli, "Defense Planning in Pakistan," in Stephanie G. Neuman, ed., Defense Planning in Less-Industrialized States: The Middle East and South Asia (Lexington, Mass.: Lexington Books, 1984), 209-38. For a discussion of the problems of evaluating the political and military role of modern weapons in the security context of major developing countries, see Rodney W. Jones and Steven A. Hildreth, Modern Weapons and Third World Powers (Boulder, Colo.: Westview Press, 1984).

9. For more extensive treatment of the subject of regional nuclear proliferation and the specific role and capabilities of Pakistan, see Rodney W. Jones, ed., Small Nuclear Forces and U.S. Security Policy: Threats and Potential Conflicts in the Middle East and South Asia (Lexington, Mass.: Lexington Books, 1984), especially chapters 1-3, 5, and 11; Rodney W. Jones, Nuclear Proliferation: Islam, the Bomb, and South Asia, Center for Strategic and International Studies, Georgetown University, The Washington Papers, no. 82, (Washington, D.C., 1981).

APPENDIX

PAKISTAN'S DEFENSE STATISTICS

Year	Population	GNP $ billion	Def. Exp. $ million	Armed Forces	Army	Infantry Divisions	Armored Divisions	Independent Brigades
1969	-	15.55	545	-	-	-	-	-
1970	128,400,000	16.00	605	324,000	300,000	11	2	1
1971	126,300,000	17.00	714	392,000	365,000	12	2	2
1972	51,300,000	4.7	405	395,000	278,000 (+90,000 POWs)	10	2	2
1973	64,800,000	8.6	509	402,000	300,000 (+55,000 POWs)	12	2	2
1974	58,760,000		713	392,000	365,000	13	2	3
1975	60,170,000	10.1	725	392,000	365,000	13	2	3
1976	72,790,000		807	428,000	400,000	14	2	3
1977	74,190,000	17.6	960	428,000	400,000	14	2	6-8
1978	76,780,000	18.5	1,180	429,000	400,000	16	2	6-8
1979	80,170,000	18.5	1,278	429,000	400,000	16	2	14
1980	82,700,000		1,422	438,600	408,000	16	2	14 + 6 reconnaissance regiments
1981	88,950,000		1,857	450,600	420,000	16	2	14 +
1982	88,950,000		1,829	478,600	450,000	16	2	18 +
1983	89,500,000	28.331	1,829	478,600	450,000	16	2	18 +
1984	92,450,000	30,859	1,873	478,600	450,000	16	2	18 + 6 armored reconnaissance regiments

Source: The Military Balance (London: International Institute for Strategic Studies), annual series from 1969-1970. Note that major discrepancies exist in the year-to-year figures compiled by the I.I.S.S. Those displayed above take later figures from the series when these appear to be firmer than those first published in the series. There are obvious anomalies in the estimated population figures between 1972 and 1976.

The Effect of the Afghan Refugees on Pakistan

Grant M. Farr

This chapter discusses the Afghan refugees in Pakistan, in particular those aspects of the refugee situation that may pose problems to the government of Pakistan in the long and short runs. I will argue that while the refugee situation has been handled well so far, and while there has been relatively little conflict, there are several issues that may spell long-term problems for Pakistan, given the size of the refugee population.

The refugee problem is in part a product of the size and nature of the Afghan refugee population, the largest refugee group in the world. Size alone creates logistical problems of providing shelter, food, water and other material needs on a very large scale. The size of the refugee population also puts serious strain on public and municipal facilities and undue pressure on the natural environment. The large number of refugees also provokes overt unrest among the native population, who feel that the quality of their own lifestyle is threatened. While these problems are great, they are perhaps not the most serious of the problems facing Pakistan. Of more concern to Pakistan and of more serious threat to its stability is what will happen if the refugees do not return to Afghanistan. If they do not return soon, and it appears that they will not, their continued presence will have important political and economic consequences both for local regions and for the country as a whole. If the refugees become permanent settlers, the parallel with the Palestinian situation is unavoidable.

While the problems facing Pakistan as a result of the massive influx of Afghan refugees are great, these problems need not threaten the stability of the government of Pakistan. Accommodating nearly three million refugees in a relatively poor country presents great difficulties, but Pakistan has undergone more traumatic events in its brief history. Unless major unexpected events take place (a Soviet invasion of Pakistan, for instance), the refugee situation will continue to be manageable in the forseeable future.

Size and Nature of the Refugee Population

Historically the 1500-mile Afghan-Pakistan border has meant little to the Pushtun tribes who live on both sides. Referred to as the Durand Line, the border was fixed between Amir Abdul Rahman Khan and Sir Mortimer Durand in 1893. The Afghans have since argued that the line was meant only to indicate spheres of influence and not national bounderies. Nonetheless, at the time of partition the Durand Line became the official boundary between Pakistan and Afghanistan, despite Afghan protests.[1] The border to this day is largely undemarcated, and the partially nomadic Pushtun tribes in that area have seasonally crossed back and forth from the mountains of Afghanistan in the summer to the warm Indus plain in the winter. To the Pushtuns, the area on both sides of the border is Pushtunistan, and the Durand Line, which cuts their area in half, has always been rejected as an artificial creation of the British. It is estimated that in the years before the beginning of the current refugee influx, approximately 75,000 Afghans crossed the border yearly.[2] In addition, it has been customary for Afghans to seek political asylum in Pakistan, or, earlier, in British India.

It was not unexpected, therefore, that as trouble began in Afghanistan in the 1970s, the Afghans would look towards the Northwest Frontier Province (NWFP) of Pakistan as a place of haven. There have been three stages of refugee flight, each corresponding to political events in Afghanistan. The first refugees began to come out in July 1973, in the period following Muhammad Daoud Khan's overthrow of the monarchy. The number of refugees was small in this period, perhaps only a few hundred. These first groups were largely political refugees, primarily religious fundamentalists who were persecuted by Daoud's regime. They fled mostly to Peshawar, and with the encouragement of the Pakistani government of Zulfiqar Ali Bhutto, began minor guerrilla activities against the government of Afghanistan. These were largely unsuccessful, but laid the groundwork for those who followed.

The second period of refugee exodus from Afghanistan began shortly after the events of April 1978, when Nur Muhammad Taraki overthrew the government of Daoud. While most Afghans greeted the new Marxist government of Afghanistan with a wait-and-see attitude, it became clear to many Afghans fairly quickly that all was not well. The Marxist government soon attempted to implement sweeping social changes in Afghanistan. While these changes were perhaps well meant, if naive, they plunged the country quickly into chaos and armed rebellion. The Taraki response to the deteriorating situation was brutal repression. It is estimated that nearly a half-million refugees. left Afghanistan at this time. Many intellectuals, university professors and upper-level bureaucrats were among the refugees, who moved primarily into the urban centers, especially Peshawar.

During this second period, the government of Pakistan was relatively unprepared, since the refugees were largely unexpected. Nonetheless, the government attempted to offer what it could by making public building available to the refugees. In the first year or so after 1978, there were no official camps, and the refugees made what arrangements they could. Most stayed close to the border in the tribal areas and made accommodations with local tribal leaders.

In April 1979, with the refugee population approaching one hundred thousand and the flow at nearly a thousand per day, Pakistan appealed to the United Nations High Commission for Refugees (UNHCR) for assistance. The UNHCR urged the Pakistani government to establish offical camps and to move the refugees away from the border, for reasons of politics and safety.

The third, and largest, refugee influx came after the Soviet invasion of Afghanistan in December 1979. For the first time the fighting affected a large segment of the population, as the Soviet Union quickly brought its troop strength up to 110,000 soldiers. Such anti-insurgent techniques as high-level saturation bombing, gas warfare and destruction of crops were employed by the Soviets. It became clear that the Soviet strategy was to depopulate the country so as to expose the insurgents and guerrillas.

Many more intellectuals and members of the educated class came out of Afghanistan in the few months after the Soviet invasion. The new government of Babrak Karmal released many who had been held in prison under the former regime in a general amnesty in January 1980. Most of those released lost little time getting out of the country, even though flight was dangerous and expensive.

Estimates of the number of Afghan refugees now in Pakistan (as of 1985) vary widely. Pakistani government estimates from the summer of 1984 put the refugee population at 2,864,806[3], but new counts are continually taking place. Other sources, particularly the UNHCR, estimate the number to be considerably lower, citing many cases of overenumeration. Since precise population counts in this area of the world do not exist even for the settled populations, it is not surprising that the exact size of the refugee population is not known. The government of Pakistan prefers to use higher estimates, as it receives international aid based on head count, and a larger number helps to dramatize the refugee problem. The

World Food Programme (WFP), for example, uses the lower figure of 1.7 million. The problem is that there is no good way to enumerate the refugee population, except at the time of initial registration when they first come out, and when rations are distributed. In both cases, the Pakistani refugee administration does not have adequate personnel to screen and register refugees, and there is great motivation on the part of the Afghans themselves to exaggerate their numbers. The more dependents a male head of household, or a village elder, can claim, the more rations he receives.[4]

In addition to the registered refugees, there are perhaps as many as 200,000 unregistered refugees who do not or cannot live in the official camps. More will be said about this group later.

How and why the refugees left is an article in itself, but some discussion is relevant here, since the reasons they left will affect the probablity of their return. The common assumption is that most of the approximately three million refugees in Pakistan have been forced from Afghanistan because of the war, that they are fleeing directly from the combat areas because of bombing or firing that directly endanger their lives and property. While partially true, this picture of the refugee situation cannot be completely accurate, because many of the refugees do not come from areas where fighting is heaviest. In fact, a large part of the countryside of Afghanistan is relatively untouched by direct fighting, at least according to the reliable observations of journalists and others, who report that one can travel relatively freely around the hinterland of Afghanistan and see little evidence of fighting.

Refugees leave for several more specific reasons: fear of conscription in the military, the loss of home or village, or economic or political reasons. Research on other acute refugee movements finds that in situations of mass flight, many who flee have little to fear, but flee because of the atmosphere of panic or hysteria.[5]

Important also are the demographic characteristics of the refugee population. Here again good estimates are hard to obtain, but by most accounts the refugee population consists mostly of women, children and older men. The share of women and children is estimated to be as high as 75 percent.[6] This very high dependency ratio adds to the burden of supplying the refugees with aid, since the needs of this group are greater. It also appears that the birthrate among refugees in the camps is high, again putting greater demand on the health care providers. Pushtuns account for 94 percent of the refugees, and 86 percent were unskilled laborers or peasants in Afghanistan.[7]

Refugee Settlement Patterns and Local Response

Most of the refugees fleeing into Pakistan come from areas near the border. These areas are largely Pushtun. As a consequence, while the Pushtuns make up only just over 50 percent of the population of Afghanistan, they account for the vast majority of the refugees. Table I shows the distribution of the refugees by province in Pakistan.

TABLE I

DISTRIBUTION OF AFGHAN REFUGEES IN PAKISTAN

Province	Camps	Population
NWFP	77	1,306,695
Tribal Areas	102	740,386
Baluchistan	60	727,173
Punjab	10	91,552
TOTAL	249	2,865,806

Source: Chief Commissioner for Afghan Refugees, Islamabad.

Most of the refugees—71 percent of the total—are in the Tribal Areas or NWFP.[8] As a consequence, these areas were closed to further registration in 1982, because the density had become too great.

By all accounts, the reception of the Afghan refugees into Pakistan has been surprisingly smooth and without violence. The potential for trouble is great, simply because of the numbers, but there have been very few cases of violence against the new refugees. This is in part because most of the refugees have moved into areas of Pakistan where the local Pakistanis are of the same ethnolinguistic group, namely Pushtuns. The Pushtun majority is largely accounted for by the fact that the Pushtuns live on the Pakistani border and thus Pakistan is the closest country of exile. In addition, Pushtun tribes have traditionally sought refuge in Pakistan. Many Pushtuns, therefore, have relatives and connections in Pakistan. Thus to a large number of Afghans, Pakistan is not completely a foreign country, and to many Pakistanis Afghans are like cousins.

Similarities aside, however, problems are growing. Since space in NWFP is being used up, the Pakistan government is attempting to establish refugee camps in provinces further away from the border, particularly the Punjab. There are good reasons for moving the refugees away from the border provinces of NWFP and Baluchistan. In the first place, it distributes the load more evenly around Pakistan, thus, in theory, not overtaxing the facilities and physical environment of any one province. Redistribution of the refugees would, it is thought, decrease concentrations of large numbers of refugees and thus lessen local hostility. It would make the distribution of services somewhat easier. Most important, it would remove the refugees from near the border and thus distance them from the war inside Afghanistan. Some refugees have settled within a few miles of the border, inviting incursions by Afghan or Soviet government forces into Pakistan.

The redistribution of refugees to provinces away from the border has gone slowly however, and is fraught with political problems. For one, while the Pakistanis in NWFP and Baluchistan are closely linked to the Afghans, culturally, linguistically and historically, this is not the case with Pakistanis in other provinces, especially in the Punjab. The Pushtuns and the Punjabis have not gotten along, and there is a long-standing, bitter ethnic rivalry. The Punjabis have historically seen the Afghans as marauding warriors from the mountains who have in the past swept down on the Indus plain to conquer. To the Afghans, especially the traditionally tribal and nomadic Pushtuns, the Punjabis are soft urban dwellers and farmers, whom they have long held in contempt. In addition, the Afghans, many of whom are from high mountainous regions, are not excited about moving to the very hot Indus plain of the Punjab, where temperatures routinely climb above 110 degrees in the summer. And they do not want to move so far from the border of their country, since many refugees do return for periods of time to farm or fight.

By mid-1984 there were 91,552 registered refugees in ten refugee tent villages (RTVs) in the Punjab. UNHCR and other officials, however, believe that it is highly doubtful that number of refugees is actually in the Punjab camps. Visits to those camps reveal that they are largely empty. Many refugees officially assigned to the RTVs in the Punjab go there to register, but do not live there, only returning periodically to receive rations.

The movement of the refugees to the Punjab has created two problems for Pakistan. First, it puts two unfriendly groups into contact, raising the specter of increased interethnic conflict. Such conflict, possibly leading to violence, may be inevitable given the volatile nature of the situation and sensitivity of the ethnic groups in question. Pakistan is made up of several antagonistic ethnolinguistic groups making the concept of nationhood uncertain. The Afghan refugees add to that problem.

Second, the question of resettling the Afghan refugees within its borders shows that the government of Pakistan is only imperfectly able to control their movement and distribution. To the credit of the government, the Afghan refugees are allowed freedom to travel in Pakistan. As a result, while the Afghans are supposed to live in the official refugee villages, there is little that the Pakistan government can do to enforce. that policy, except through the distribution of rations. Repeated attempts to resettle the refugees have had only partial success, with many refugees living outside the official camps.

The distribution of the refugees will continue to be a major problem. The government of Pakistan wants to move the refugees further away from the border and especially away from the area around Peshawar where the concentration is greatest. The UNHCR and volunteer aid organizations also desire such a transfer. However, the refugees do not want to move, and the people in the other areas of Pakistan do not want them.

Refugees and Ethnic Politics
<u>Refugees and Ethnic Politics</u>

Internal ethnic divisions in Pakistan have been an important obstacle to stability since its founding. Today ethnic nationalism issues loom as a major stumbling block to long-term stability. Pakistan has historically been dominated by the Punjab; Punjabis dominate in government and the military and are expanding in business. The other major ethnic groups have long resented this domination, and separatist movements have taken place in all of the non-Punjabi provinces, especially among the Sindhis, the Baluchis and the Pushtuns.[9] The Afghan refugees complicate the picture and exacerbate these divisions.

These ethnic and regional tensions arise partly as a consequence of the uneven development of Pakistan. The Punjab and some areas of Sind are the most developed regions; Baluchistan is the least. Pakistan has attempted to resolve these imbalances through such things as a national quota for public jobs,[10] and by pouring money into development projects, especially in Baluchistan[11]. It is feared that the addition of the refugees, who themselves are highly sensitive to ethnic and tribal differences, will shift the precarious balance that has been painstakingly achieved. This, however, has not taken place so far, and seems unlikely to do so for reasons that follow.

The two provinces with the most refugees have not seen an increase of regionalist movements since the refugee influx. In NWFP, Pushtun nationalism has periodically been a political force and is always near the surface. Although it might have been expected that the addition of over 1.3 million fellow Pushtuns would increase Pushtun nationalist sentiments, this has not been the case. This is in part because the Afghan Pushtuns have a somewhat different version of Pushtun nationalism than do the

Pakistani Pushtuns. Despite protestations that there are no differences between Pushtuns living in Pakistan and those coming from Afghanistan, in fact serious differences do exist. Besides differences of dialect and tribal customs, the Pushtuns in Pakistan have lived on the margin of countries run by other peoples. First in British India and now in Pakistan, they are a minority living on a frontier some distance from the center of power.

The Afghan Pushtuns, on the contrary, have been the dominant group in Afghanistan. The history of the rulers of Afghanistan is the history of the Pushtuns. To the Afghan Pushtuns, the issue of Pushtun nationalism is an old one that involves freeing the territory where the Pushtuns live, Pushtunistan, from Pakistan. It is a much larger issue to the Afghan Pushtuns than to the Pakistani Pushtuns, who see the issue more in terms of settling economic issues with Islamabad. As a consequence, the Afghan refugees have not greatly increased Pushtun nationalism in NWFP.

Numbers may play a part here, too. The population of NWFP is 14.6 million, not counting the refugees.[12] The refugees represent an increase of 1.3 million, or about 9 percent. This is a significant increase but not large enough to have a great effect on ethnic politics. Another factor is that at this time the focus of the Afghans is on Afghanistan and the war to drive out the Marxists. They have largely stayed out of regional politics up to now.

The situation in Baluchistan is somewhat different. In the first place, there have been more serious demands for greater provincial autonomy in Baluchistan. The population of Baluchistan is 3.25 million,[13] considerably smaller than NWFP. Baluchistan is also by far the poorest of Pakistan's provinces. The strategy of the Zia government here has been to put money into development projects that will create jobs, and to buy off tribal sardars (local landlords) with promises of projects.[14]

The ethnic tensions that the refugees bring to Baluchistan are somewhat different than in NWFP. The Baluchis have long resented the domination of the Pushtun tribes in their area. Quetta, the capital of Baluchistan, is heavily Pushtun, and now with the influx of mostly Pushtun refugees, the province threatens to develop a Pushtun majority, if it is not already. These tensions are still relatively unfocused and not yet a problem. However, the potential for trouble is present. Given the strategic importance of the area, many expect that Soviet agents may try to stir up trouble there, creating a situation that they might exploit and thus gain access to the Persian Gulf. Zia, on the other hand, seems well aware of the potential problems in Baluchistan and has acted wisely. Given five years in which to stir up trouble, the Soviets have done nothing visible.[15]

Economic Issues

Physically, the refugees are well taken care of. The government of Pakistan, and many world agencies including the UNHCR, the World Food Programme, the International Committee of the Red Cross (ICRC), the United Nations Children's Fund (UNICEF) and others are working to provide the refugees with food, shelter, water and medical care. The government of Pakistan, through the Commissioner for Refugees, administers rations of wheat, cooking and heating oil, meat and even cash. While these resources are sometimes slow in coming, especially the cash, and even though much of the cost is met by the UNHCR and other groups, they represent nonetheless a considerable expense for Pakistan. While the physical conditions in the camps may not be up to Western standards, they are good by local standards. Camp life may be better physically than was life in Afghanistan and perhaps better physically than the life of a local Pakistani farmer.

There is, however, a growing concern about the quality of the life of the refugees. There is a fear that they are beginning to develop a "welfare" mentality, coming to expect aid rather than earning it themselves. The role of women in the Afghan refugee community has worsened, given the restrictive living conditions. In addition, there has been a deterioration in the traditional Afghan social structure, and a new kind of social organization is emerging among the refugee community. Where the old social organization was based on the realities of rural tribal society, organized around kinship, and the economics of farming and herding, the new social organization is based around the realities of camp life. Because of the problems of dealing with a foreign government, and the problems not of producing a living from the soil as in Afghanistan, but of dealing with the complicated Pakistani bureaucracy, "socio-political institutions, though still recognizable as Afghan, have skewed away from traditional patterns."[16]

A new kind of leader has developed as part of this new structure. While the traditional village and tribal leaders still have much power, the new leadership reflects the reality of camp life. These "ration maliks" are able to deal with the Pakistani bureaucracy, able to get extra ration cards, and, in general, able to deal with the new realities of camp life.[17]

One of the strategies used by the government of Pakistan and the UNHCR to counter these undesirable developments has been to develop projects that will employ the refugees and allow them to earn income. This is a two-edged sword. On the one hand, it is seen as desirable for the refugees to work; it increases self-sufficiency and self-esteem, decreasing dependency on charity. The camp life in general is debilitating. Fathers are no longer teaching their sons their traditional crafts and skills, since they are not required in camp life. The Pakistanis especially worry that idle hands may turn to political intrigue and mischief.

On the other hand, refugees who are economically active may be less likely to return to Afghanistan when the fighting stops, especially if their jobs are in the local economy. Those who have found and settled in good jobs will not necessarily be willing to return. In addition, Pakistan itself has a labor surplus and every Afghan employed potentially takes a job away from a Pakistani, and thus increases local hostility.

Consequently, the emphasis has been on self-contained refugee projects that provide the refugees work and self-sufficiency and diverts their energies, but do not take jobs from local Pakistanis nor encourage the refugees to put down roots. These efforts have not been very successful, and most of the refugees lack skills or interest in these projects. The International Labor Organization (ILO) has started a vegetable seed project, and some "truck farming" projects have had success on a small scale. The Small Industry Development Board (SIBD), an agency of the Pakistan Refugee Commission, along with the UNHCR, has begun a carpet-weaving center in Dargamandi, in North Waziristan. The project has proved to be moderately successful among certain ethnic groups, especially the Turkomans, Uzbeks and Tajiks, who traditionally make carpets in Afghanistan. The Pushtuns, who make up 94 percent of the refugees, do not make carpets, however, and do not participate in the project, limiting drastically its scope.[18]

Attempts to keep the refugees out of the local Pakistani economy may be too little and too late. Two 1982 internal UNHCR reports make several points with regard to the economic participation of the Afghan refugees. In a survey done in refugee camps in the Kohat district, 72 percent of the adult males had some type of employment that brought in wages, and 87 percent of the families had at least one wage-earning member of the household.[19] The refugees were engaged in the following occupations:[20]

1. Kitchen-gardening in fruits, vegetables and spices;
2. Officially employed by the government of Pakistan to work in areas of reforestation, water drainage, etc.;
3. Farming land leased from local Pakistani peasants;
4. Daily labor, especially in the labor-intensive marketplaces in the large urban centers;
5. Trade and smuggling, especially drugs and arms;
6. Trucking and shipping;
7. Livestock;
8. Merchants and craftsmen.

Trucking and shipping deserves more comment since they play important roles and supply work for many. As new roads were built in Afghanistan in the 1960s and 1970s, traditional traders began to motorize their business. At the same time, West Germany liberalized its export credit for Afghanistan, and many heavy and light trucks were brought into the country. Many of the refugees bring their trucks with them as they flee Afghanistan. Pakistani authorities have been registering these vehicles under temporary registration and allowing the Afghans to continue to work. This Pakistani policy is due to the fact that Pakistan has an acute shortage of heavy trucks.

In NWFP alone, there are 893 heavy trucks, 55 large buses, 173 minibuses, 152 tractors, 411 cars, cabs, jeeps and pick-ups, and 21 motorcycles or rickshaws—totaling 1705 vehicles—registered to refugees. There are probably as many more unregistered. Each of these provides a living for one or more families. For instance, it usually takes several adult men to operate and maintain a large truck, and each man supports a family of several people. In total, it is estimated that 60,000 Afghan refugee families are supported from the motorized transport business in NWFP and in the rest of Pakistan.[21] In addition the UNHCR estimates that 45,000 camels and 25,000 donkeys are owned by Afghan refugees in Pakistan.[22] These animals are used for commercial purposes in Pakistan and bring income to refugee families.

The Afghans have also begun small retail shops in several urban centers and along major highways. Usually very small, and selling only inexpensive items, these shops are nonetheless gaining a foothold in the bazaars of Peshawar and Islamabad. Many Afghans are also working as craftsmen. The Afghans have made great inroads into the tailoring business in Peshawar and are considered the best tailors of traditional clothes.

In sum, the Afghan refugees have already penetrated the Pakistani economy in a major way. This will continue to create serious problems for the Pakistan government. At the present time, the problem is somewhat reduced since many Pakistani men work abroad. It is estimated that there are 3.5 million Pakistanis working outside Pakistan, mainly in Middle Eastern countries, and that these workers remit nearly $2 billion yearly to Pakistan.[23] Some of this money is then privately invested in small infrastructural arrangements, construction and luxury goods that in turn create jobs in Pakistan. Afghan refugees therefore move into the jobs that the manpower shortage creates.

On the other hand, the economic activity of the Afghan refugee represents a time bomb. Many of the overseas Pakistani laborers will return, and competition for jobs will increase. The surplus of labor will inevitably lead to a lowering of wages and thus to a lower standard of living for most workers. Even now Afghan labor is cheaper than equivalent Pakistani labor. Resentment among local Pakistanis will grow. While the government of Pakistan may welcome the Afghan trucks, what the local Pakistani sees is that the trucking business is being taken over by Afghans, who charge lower rates, and who, as refugees, are exempt from the same licensing fees as refugees.

Unregistered Refugees

Although most of the focus of this chapter has been on the refugees who live in the camps, there are actually several kinds of refugees in exile in Pakistan. The refugees who live in the official camps are primarily peasants, Pushtu speakers, coming from either rural villages or nomadic tribes. There are, however, many refugees who cannot or will not live in the camps. They are of two kinds: non-Pushtun ethnic groups who feel that they cannot live in the largely Pushtun-dominated camps, and former middle class Kabul residents. The former are primarily Tajiks, Hazaras and Turkomans, whose ethnic antagonism towards the dominant Pushtuns is old and deep.[24] The refugees who do not live in the camps account for perhaps 5 percent of the refugee population. They live mostly in the border cities of Peshawar and Quetta, but many also have moved to Islamabad and Karachi. The refugees who do not live in the offical camps are denied full refugee status, primarily the rights to receive rations of food and other goods. The Pakistan government, in agreement with UNHCR, has ruled that a refugee must live in the camps to receive full benefits. While this decision has some wisdom, it creates physical hardship for those refugees who feel that they cannot live in the camps.

Some of the non-Pushtun ethnic groups were also peasant farmers in Afghanistan, mainly the Hazaras and Tajiks, and thus left Afghanistan for the reasons stated above. Other groups, especially the Turkomans, were traditional merchants, bazaar-keepers, traders and middlemen. The Turkomans, for instance, traditionally brought carpets from the north of Afghanistan to Kabul for market. Now they bring their carpets to Peshawar and Islamabad, since Kabul is isolated from the world market. Some of these non-Pushtun groups do live in camps, but in general they prefer not to do so, either because the camps are dominated by Pushtuns or because those camps set up for the non-Pushtun groups are in undesirable places.

Both the UNHCR and the Pakistan Refugee Commissioner's office have largely ignored ethnic differences among the refugees, viewing the refugees as a rather homogeneous population. Ethnic divisiveness is not now an important item in the minds of the Afghans; they are more concerned about the occupation of their country and the war to drive out the Soviets. Nonetheless, unless Pakistan and the other policy-making organizations exercise some understanding of the important ethnic, linguistic and racial differences among the refugees themselves, these issues could well become explosive as the attention of the refugees begins to turn from Afghanistan to Pakistan.

Another group of refugees not living in the camps are the urban dwellers, primarily from Kabul. Although small in number, perhaps only a few thousand, they were members of the emergent Afghan middle class. They were often bureaucrats in Kabul working in the large Afghan government agencies, or teachers, university professors and merchants. They are more important than their numbers indicate, since they are the literate and possess skills important to a developing country. They will not or cannot live in the camps, in part because they no longer have the tribal or village connections around which camp life is based, and because camp life represents the type of traditional rural life from which their recent upward mobility has allowed them to escape. Because they do not live in the camps, they do not receive rations and must therefore pay their own expenses for housing and other living costs. Many live in substandard housing. Those who can migrate to the U.S. or Europe. Because few of those who go to Europe or America will ever return to Afghanistan, this outflow of the educated class represents a significant brain drain. It leaves both a future Afghanistan and the refugee community in Pakistan without an educated class.

Among these urban refugees from Kabul are a rather large group of single men in their late teens or early twenties. Many of them have fled Kabul or other urban centers to avoid military conscription. They have often been sent out alone by their families. Many have graduated from high school. They are largely Dari speakers, the Afghan variant of Persian, and many speak a European language, usually French or English, learned in high school. They live in the urban centers of Peshawar and Islamabad, often many in a single room. They are potentially the most restive of all of the refugees, despite their small number. Being in the urban areas, they are the most visible to the local Pakistanis. Largely unemployed and not having families, they tend to congregate in urban public places. As a consequence, they arouse the suspicion of the Pakistanis, and are accused of all types of mischief.

These youths also represent an important, although yet unrealized, political force. They are generally well informed about political issues and articulate in expressing their views. They could easily become an important political power, since they are not otherwise occupied. But this time their political interests are diffuse and unfocused.

Refugee Repatriation

Of great concern to Pakistan and to the Afghan refugees as well is the question of repatriation: Will the refugees return, and under what conditions? Although it has been five years since the Soviet invasion and twelve years since the first trickling of refugees started, the government of Pakistan has managed to defuse local hostility by operating as if the situation were temporary. As long as most of the people believe that the Afghans will soon depart, they will suffer in relative silence. This is not a deception, since the government of Pakistan firmly hopes and believes that an arrangement can soon be worked out so that the refugees might return to Afghanistan.

Time is working against this strategy, as it begins to become apparent that the Afghans are not going back in the short run, and that indeed the short run has become the long run. The reasons that the Afghans will probably not return soon are several, and include the lack of progress on an international agreement between the principal countries that would end the fighting, the penetration of the Afghans into Pakistan's economy, and the passage of time itself.

History teaches us that as more time passes, fewer refugees will return. Studies on refugee movements divide the time into roughly four periods: the first year or so when the trauma and bitterness of the recent tragic events overwhelm other feelings; the next two or three years when the refugee works with particular vigor to maintain contact and connections with the original country; a period of depression and feeling of hopelessness; and finally, after roughly a decade, the resignation to living in the host country.[25] Most agree that the period of four or five years marks an important watershed. As the refugee situation continues beyond this period, the likelihood that the refugee has become too deeply integrated into Pakistani society grows, the loss of contact with the situation in Afghanistan increases, the refugee ages, and the children are entering Pakistani schools. Camp life is becoming routine, and the expectation of returning decreases. In addition, the new kind of leader mentioned above emerges in the camps, one whose power no longer depends on the traditional tribal or village structure. These men have little to gain by encouraging their people to return, since their power comes from the camp environment.

Time then is growing short. As time passes and the refugees do not return, the problems for Pakistan increase. One problem will be to maintain the level of assistance that will be required to maintain more or less permanent camps. Here the world community, especially the U.S., will probably maintain its level of support. Another problem will be the political and social unrest that will likely increase when the Pakistani citizen sees that the Afghans are not leaving. Already many of the municipal services of cities affected most by the refugees are stretched to the limit. Buses are full, services strained, bazaars and streets crowded and tempers are beginning to flare. At first the Pakistani press was quiet on the refugee issue, but more and more they discuss the "refugee problem." It is becoming a major issue of discussion in Pakistan. Afghan refugees are increasingly being blamed for anything and everything that goes wrong. Stories abound of Afghans attacking Pakistani women, of Afghans robbing Pakistanis, of Afghans driving Pakistanis from their jobs or homes. Nobody claims the Afghans are perfect people, but they are being blamed for much of the trouble in Pakistan now, because they are an easy scapegoat in a country with many frustrations.

In addition, as time passes and the Afghans do not return, they will increasingly become a political force in Pakistan. Even now, the Afghans in Pakistan operate as largely independent political organizations outside the direct control of the government. At this date, the Afghan political parties are largely concerned with the war in Afghanistan, but several of the parties are closely allied with the Pakistani conservative religious groups, especially the Jamaat-i-Islami. The government's main method of control over the Afghan groups is through its control of arms and other material necessary for the war. As time passes, their interest will increasingly turn toward issues in Pakistan. The Afghan refugees will be used by Pakistani political groups, and the Afghans will in turn increasingly exercise political power in Pakistan.

The Afghan political groups are largely religious and conservative. They therefore affiliate with the conservative, religious Pakistani political groups. There are, however, other ideological groups among the Afghans, including secular nationalists and nonaligned Marxists. For the time being, with religious elements dominating Pakistan's politics, the political participation of the equally religious and conservative Afghan groups is not an issue in national politics.

Conclusion

The Afghan refugees pose many problems in Pakistan. At this time, they are more potential problems than actual problems. There is the potential for economic competition between the Afghans and the Pakistani workers and shopkeepers. The Afghans may exacerbate ethnic tensions and stir up nationalism in the provinces. There is the possibility that the refugees will become entangled in the politics of Pakistan, tipping the balance one way or the other. And there is the probability that if the Afghans do not soon return to their homeland, they will take on semipermanent status, much like the Palestinians in Lebanon and Jordan, creating a similar situation.

These problems aside, Pakistan has done an admirable job in the last five years. There has been little violence. There have been virtually no cases of starvation or outbreaks of disease. There is an attempt to employ the Afghans. Many world agencies are now in Pakistan to assist with refugee aid. In short, there is no reason to believe that the government of Pakistan will not continue to deal effectively with the Afghan refugee situation.

There are many potential problems, but it has now been twelve years since refugees first started coming and five years since the Soviet invasion. The short run has become the long run, and the government of Pakistan has demonstrated that so far it can manage the situation.

NOTES

1. For a good discussion of the British/Afghan relations at that time see Louis Dupree, Afghanistan (Princeton: Princeton University Press, 1980), 426–27.

2. Beverly Male, "A Tiger by the Tail: Pakistan and the Afghan Refugees," in Milton Osborne et al., Refugees: Four Political Case Studies (Canberra: The Australian National University Press, 1981), 39.

3. Report from Chief Commissioner for Afghan Refugees, Islamabad, Pakistan, August 1983.

4. For a good discussion of the numbers game and multiple registration ploys see Nancy Hatch Dupree, "The Demography of Afghan Refugees in Pakistan" (Paper delivered at a seminar, Pakistan, Iran and Afghanistan in Soviet-American Relations, Villanova University, Villanova, December 8, 1984).

5. Barry Stein, "The Refugee Experience: Defining the Parameters of a Field of Study," International Migration Review 15, no. 6 (Summer 1981): 322.

6. Nancy Hatch Dupree, "Demography," 27, 28.

7. United Nations High Commission for Refugees, internal report (Peshawar: September 1982).

8. The tribal areas are semi-independent areas where Pushtun tribes still control their own affairs to some degree.

9. For a good discussion of the ethnic problems in Pakistan see Charles H. Kennedy, "Policies of Ethnic Preference in Pakistan," Asian Survey 29, no. 6 (June 1984): 688-703, and Khalid Bin Sayeed, "Pakistan in 1983: Internal Stresses More Serious Than External Problems," Asian Survey 24, no. 2 (February 1984): 219-28.

10. Kennedy, "Ethnic Preference," 691.

11. Sayeed, "Pakistan in 1983," 224.

12. Kennedy, "Ethnic Preference," 689.

13. Ibid.

14. Sayeed, "Pakistan in 1983," 224.

15. For a further discussion of the Baluchistan situation see Selig Harrison, In Afghanistan's Shadow: Baluch Nationalism and Soviet Temptation (Washington, D.C.: Carnegie Endowment for International Peace, 1980).

16. Louis Dupree, "Afghanistan in 1983: And Still No Solution," Asian Survey 24, no. 2 (February 1984): 233.

17. For a slightly different discussion of this, see Louis Dupree, "No Solution," 233. He talks of three type of maliks; the "traditional" malik, the "self-made" malik, who is the same as my "ration" malik, and the mujahidin commander who gains prestige by fighting.

18. Marcel Ackerman, "Self-Reliance/Income Generating of Afghan Refugees in NWFP," Memo to Chief of Sub-office, Pakistan (Peshawar: September 1982).

19. Marie Sardie and Mamoona Taskinud-din, "Nutrition Status, Socio-economic Factors," (Peshawar: UNHCR, September 1982).

20. Ackerman, "Self-Reliance," 1-5.

21. Ibid.

22. Ibid.

23. See Fred Arnold and Nasra Shah, "Asian Labor Migration to the Middle East," International Migration Review 18, no. 2 (Summer 1984): 294-318. Also Jonathan Addleton, "The Impact of International Migration on Economic Development in Pakistan," Asian Survey 24, no. 5 (May 1984): 574-96.

24. Those who say that the present situation in Afghanistan has united the various ethnic groups are wrong; traditional antagonisms remain, appearances to the contrary.

25. For a good discussion of the issues involved in refugee repatriation see Barry N. Stein, "The Commitment to Refugee Resettlement," Annals, American Academy of Political and Social Science, (May 1983): 187-201.

Conclusion: Legitimacy for Zia and His Regime?

Craig Baxter

The transforming regime of President Muhammad Zia ul-Haq has survived for nearly eight years. To survive, Zia has drawn on many of the tools which are available to nonrepresentative regimes. He has also been the beneficiary of a surprisingly high level of good fortune. However, he must now work for something much more substantial and more difficult to obtain than survival: legitimacy for his government, his regime and the political community of Pakistan.[1] The papers in this study have detailed the task Zia has accomplished, that is, survival. They have also set forth the base upon which he must build if he is to achieve legitimacy at each of the three levels toward which legitimacy can be directed.

Legitimacy

Zia first wishes to attain legitimacy for himself and his government, for "the authorities" in David Easton's term.[2] He has seen how legitimacy cannot be attained, and, if he had looked at the earlier record of Pakistani and Bangladeshi leaders, he might have avoided the questionable referendum of December 1984. Muhammad Ayub Khan used a referendum in his Basic Democracies scheme to regularize his holding of the presidential office. But this did not confer legitimacy on Ayub; that would come only when his regime displayed that it was effective in governing the nation. When it was clear that Ayub's government was no longer effective, the legitimacy was lost and he and his government were dislodged from office.*

---

*General Ziaur Rahman, president of Bangladesh, also used the referendum technique, asking for approval of his rule and his

111

The principal element in the failure of referenda to confer legitimacy on either Ayub or Zia ul-Haq is the absence on the ballot of any alternative to the person and program of the ruler asking for confirmation. What would have happened had the voters recorded a resounding negative vote in the referendum in December, assuming such a result would have been announced? Possibly Zia would have resigned, but another military officer probably would have replaced Zia and reversed any of the minimal political gains that Zia had granted up to that point. Zia has taken the favorable vote as a mandate for his own presidency for a new period of five years. This, too, is an unwarranted conclusion and could be upset if the new national legislative body is permitted to function as a parliamentary group which can actually exercise powers to amend the constitution. Zia's position, as a result of the referendum, could actually be more precarious than it would have been without it. The new assembly might well have chosen Zia as president, especially with the knowledge that the military wished such a result.

Zia seems to wish to change the relationship between the president and the prime minister mandated by the 1973 constitution. Under that document, the president was under the effective control of the prime minister and the cabinet; he could take no official act without the approval of the cabinet. The amendments Zia has decreed are a return to the viceregal system of the Government of India Act of 1935, under which Pakistan was governed until 1958, with some amendments pertaining to the independence of the country in 1947. Using these powers the governors general and president, with an interlude between the death of Muhammad Ali Jinnah (1949) and the assassination of Liaquat Ali Khan (1951), were able to dismiss cabinets and even dissolve the assembly and eventually dismiss the regime through the proclamation of martial law in 1958. In his announced amendments to the 1973 constitution, Zia has reserved for the president the right to dismiss the National Assembly on his own

---

*(continued) program in 1977. He won overwhelmingly, as did Zia ul-Haq, but he found that the vote did not legitimize his rule or regime. One problem was that no alternative to Ziaur Rahman was present. Ziaur Rahman followed this with a contested presidential election in 1978 and party-contested parliamentary elections in 1979. These elections presented alternatives to the voters and served, along with effective governance (in the Bangladesh context), to legitimize the government and regime of Ziaur Rahman. The present Bangladeshi ruler, General H.M. Ershad, has also used the referendum technique, no doubt also failing thereby to gain legitimacy.

initiative. At the same time, he has made the process of further amendment more difficult by requiring a two-thirds majority vote in both the Senate and National Assembly, as well as a simple majority vote in each of the provincial assemblies.

The Zia-prescribed regime will, when it becomes effective, have another safeguard which will perpetuate military control and permit the military to intervene when it deems necessary. The creation of a National Security Council is modeled after the Turkish constitution (Article III of that document). The eleven-man council will include the president, the prime minister, the chairman of the Senate, the chairman of the Joint Chiefs of Staff, the three service chiefs of staff, and the four chief ministers of the provinces.[3] Assuming the presidency is filled by a retired military officer, there will be five military representatives and six civilians. The power of the president to change the prime minister, and the power of the governors (who, for the time being at least, are military men) to dismiss the chief ministers, however, leaves only the chairman of the Senate as a fully independent actor (and he, Ghulam Ishaque Khan, was for years a close associate of Zia as the principal economic minister in the cabinet). The council is to be merely an advisory body, but, coupled with the new designation of the president as supreme commander of the armed forces, it is unlikely that its advice will be ignored. Zia, by two moves, has thus accomplished one of his goals: the constitutional guarantee of a role for the military in the governance of Pakistan.

Participation and Legitimacy

The creation of the National Security Council and the power of the president to dismiss the national assembly on his own initiative (the modified Senate will remain as a continuing body not subject to constitutional dissolution) together limit severely the declared object of legislative sovereignty. It is possible for the legislature to amend the constitution, but it can be expected that proposals for sharp changes would invoke the "advice" of the National Security Council if they had not already invited presidential dissolution.

Despite the strange position in which the voters found themselves not knowing for what they were voting, the turnout in the February 1985 election was quite high by Pakistani standards. The amendments were announced after the polling was over. The unofficial, but announced, percentage of participation was as follows:

Province	National	Provincial
The Punjab	59.59	61.80
Sind	44.60	49.82
Northwest Frontier	38.81	47.61
Tribal Areas	75.00	—
Baluchistan	35.13	46.62
Capital Area	60.24	—
Total	52.93	56.91

When these are compared with the turnout at the December 1984 referendum, they are markedly higher than the 10 to 15 percent some press reports claimed,[4] although lower than the clearly inflated government claim of 62 percent. The participation can also be compared with that in the equally well-run 1970 election; the differences are slight. The provincial variations can be explained by historic patterns in which the Punjab has led in turnout, and the other provinces have followed in the same order as they did in this election. It is also interesting that the few days between the national and provincial elections have apparently brought out a few more voters. There have been some allegations of ballot box stuffing in the provincial elections, charges which are all but absent in the national poll. A more likely explanation may be that the smaller constituencies gave the electorate a greater familiarity with the candidates.

Participation which breeds legitimacy cannot be measured only by voter turnouts. In these elections, the electorate was not only voting blind as to the powers of those elected, but was also denied the opportunity to select among party platforms, among alternative policy options. While some candidates were clearly recognizable for their views and their membership in "defunct" political parties, most appear to have been without previous identification and thus without clearly framed and publicly proclaimed national or provincial policy positions. Observers have tried to tally the results with previous party membership, but at this writing the results of such analysis are at best doubtful. For example, The Times of London reported that 38 of those elected to the National Assembly had been members of Bhutto's Pakistan People's party (PPP), 42 were associated with the right-of-center Muslim League led by the Pir of Pagaro, and nine came from the fundamentalist Jamaat-i-Islami.[5]

Zia, by holding nonpartisan elections, is consciously or otherwise following a path Ayub tried in his first (indirect) elections to the assemblies in 1962. It failed for Ayub; the members of the assemblies (national and provincial) divided into the king's party and the opposition early on. Ayub yielded and permitted parties to be formed. Zia may well find that he must do the same. His new changes in the constitution did not eliminate the provisions pertaining to political parties. In his speech of March 2, 1985, he said that a decision on party formation or the continuance of nonparty politics would be made by the National Assembly and the Senate (which together will be termed the Majlis-i-Shura).

Many of the religious scholars who gave advice, solicited and unsolicited, to Zia on the form of government opposed political parties. The basis for this was the common belief that the Muslim community (ummah) must not unite in error. Thus, in the view of many religious specialists, the existence of parties would indicate divisions, and thus error, within the Islamic community.

Nonetheless, it would seem likely that divisions, if not actual parties, are inevitable. The new prime minister, Muhammad Khan Junejo, however, did receive unanimous support when he sought a vote of confidence. The prime minister (and the president) must look to coalition building, as in any political system, and in doing so they must find a combination which will give support willingly based on its demands being met effectively by the government.

All of these aspects of Zia's newly modified regime may or may not stand the test of time. He will undoubtedly work hard to preserve the transformation of Pakistan he has accomplished so far, including the Islamization program, and to do it in a framework which is set out in his new amendments to the constitution. This, too, will require careful coalition building. However, before we turn to coalition building and the place of the groups studied in the papers, we must look briefly at Zia's record on the third object of legitimacy.

Legitimacy and the Political Community

Besides the authorities and the regime, we need to consider briefly the record on the critical matter of nation building (or creating legitimacy for the political community) in Pakistan. The record has not been one of success. The unity of the state was broken when Bangladesh separated in 1971. But the complaint of Punjabi dominance which is heard in the smaller provinces and which existed in West Pakistan before 1971 has become, since 1971, a much sharper matter than it was earlier. It is not a solution to the problem to anger the mobile and economically aggressive Punjabis. It has been suggested, in fact, that the mobility displayed by the Punjabis and, to a lesser but significant degree, by the Pathans and the Baluch has done much to weld Pakistan into a single economic and demographic unit. It is interesting to note that the new amendments to the constitution have incorporated the 1949 Objectives Resolution of the

Constituent Assembly which declares Pakistan will be an Islamic federal republic. (With these and earlier amendments, a careful editing of the constitution as it now stands will surely be needed!)

The grievances are most strongly expressed now by the Sindhis, the group which appears to be the least mobile. It is their province into which others move (although the Punjabis move anywhere as opportunity allows). It is also in Sind that the refugees (muhajirin) from India have had the greatest impact in commerce and the professions. These grievances have swelled into violence in areas of Sind. Zia and his regime have not successfully met the complaints of the Sindhis. On the other hand, it is not clear what can be done. Karachi is a cosmopolitan city and a seaport, and expelling non-Sindhis is not a reasonable step. Nor would it be possible to ban further investment and employment of persons from outside Sind; bans on movement have been a political device to halt the travels of opposition politicians but not to stifle economically useful investment.

Unlike Bhutto, Zia has followed a policy of using the carrot rather than the stick in both Baluchistan and the Northwest Frontier Province (NWFP). The development needs of each province, especially Baluchistan, are great and difficult to meet. The Baluch probably already are a minority in their own province with Frontier migrants of long standing occupying much of the north and the city of Quetta, and more recently Punjabis moving in. NWFP (and to a lesser extent Baluchistan) has large numbers of Afghan refugees, who seem unlikely to be able to return to Afghanistan in the foreseeable future, and who will have to be absorbed into the province.

The international climate also has a bearing on the unity of Pakistan. Economic problems are alleviated to a degree by the opportunities presented for employment in the Middle East, but these opportunities could shrink as oil revenues decline or as projects are completed. This would raise the level of competition for jobs and aggravate provincial complaints. The Soviet invasion of Afghanistan has probably lessened provincial rivalries as the "atheist Soviets" are less likely to be acceptable to all but the most ardent separatists. India, too, will have a bearing on Sindhi problems; it is probable that India had some role in the Sind disturbances if only that the statements of Indira Gandhi on democracy and self-determination gave some encouragement to the demonstrators. The international environment, however, is something over which Zia and his government have little control, although working toward an acceptable settlement of the Afghan issue and moving further toward improved relations with India could help.

Coalition Building

In the name of survival, Zia has placed restrictions on political behavior, rewarded some groups in the political community, and governed with the support of the military, at times in conflict with the people. He has now gone beyond these techniques by proclaiming a modified participatory and partially democratic regime. He was unable fully to ignore "politics" in the past, although by holding coercive power he has been able to act as he wishes within very broad limits. He will now presumably have to play "politics" in a much more conventional way. To do so he and his prime minister and cabinet will be required to satisfy groups within the political system in a sufficient manner that willing acceptance of him and the regime can be assured. This study has detailed the roles and attitudes of a wide range of groups toward Zia in the past and may be predictive of their views in the future.

Zia has wished to transform Pakistani society as well as establish a new regime in the political sense. His goals of Islamization surely have not been fully met. However, in a recent interview in the Christian Science Monitor, he said that he had not been "swayed by anyone, either the fundamentalists or the moderates. I form my own opinions. And I, myself, am a moderate."[6] There are several unanswered questions about Islamization. Does Zia feel that his steps so far are the key ones and that further Islamization may not be needed? Did he expect the fundamentalist parties, especially the Jamaat-i-Islami, to win a larger number of seats in the National Assembly, and thus spearhead the drive toward Islamization in that body rather than in the presidential office? Would Zia tolerate steps "backward" from Islamization? Would it be possible to go back even if conditions appear to dictate a relaxation of, say, Islamic banking? It would seem that this is an area in which Zia's steps are not complete if the fundamentalist view is taken as his, but he has denied this in his interview.

The groups which have been studied almost all seem to give Zia some support, but it is neither unqualified nor necessarily permanent.

-- The upper classes, both rural and urban, landed, economic and administrative, are often the groups which will go along with almost any regime with the intent to benefit and perhaps dominate it. The landlords may be the archetypical group; they have worked with all rulers from the Moghuls on and even went some distance in accommodating Zulfiqar Ali Bhutto as can be seen in the Pakistan People's party (PPP) candidate list for 1977.

-- The economic elites appear to be still somewhat uncertain that the climate for investment in the private sector has really changed under Zia, but clearly he is seen as a better bet than a return to Bhuttoism.

— The military rules, and could be unhappy if its powers are sharply curtailed; the National Security Council is an important gesture toward assuring military support for the regime. But this is a long way off for more junior officers. They must question what will be their future if lucrative Middle East and civil administrative posts are no longer available.

— Civil servants who have been displaced in policymaking and advisory posts may look upon the new system as a way to return to key posts, but democracy, if carried too far in the eyes of many military and civil bureaucrats, is not necessarily an advantageous system for them.

— The middle farmers have done well under Zia but not because of Zia. They will watch to see if prices remain high and markets open.

The greatest danger to Zia, as it was to Ayub, will be an economic downturn. Almost all of the groups discussed in the papers would look upon the government and the regime as the cause of poorer economic conditions. As mentioned earlier, the causes could be completely outside the control of Zia — drying up of Middle Eastern employment, weather-related problems, poor markets for cotton and basmati rice, inability of the refugees to return—but the government will get the blame.

Zia, therefore, must quickly put some credit in his account of legitimacy with as many groups as possible. He must be seen as one who tries to meet the demands of politically active groups, especially those who can be organized sufficiently to make effective their claims on the resources of Pakistan. The greater the credit available to him, the more likely it will be that he and his regime can ride out a storm.

Possible Scenarios

The new Zia regime, when it is fully implemented, will change Pakistan from a military regime to one which is not completely civilian, retaining an integral role, potential rather than actual, for the military. There are four possible scenarios: (1) military government, (2) a civilian facade with an active military role, (3) a civilian government with the military in the background but with a legal potential to intervene, and (4) a civilian government. In the last case the military would have no legal right to intervene, but could anyway, since that is always a possibility in Pakistan.

The most likely of the four scenarios probably is the second: an active military role in a government which has a civilian prime minister and elected legislative bodies. Zia may surrender his uniform, as he has stated he will, but his continuing connections with the military make the role of the military an active one. The existence of the National Security Council clinches this argument. It is not necessary to have Zia himself as the link, as Zia perforce will leave the scene. When that happens another serving or retired military officer would be his likely successor.

The second most likely scenario may well be a return to military rule. The power delegated to the National Security Council almost ensures that a change, if the council decided it were needed, would be in the direction of a return to martial law. It might be a government headed by Zia, or it might be headed by another, but military it would be. This would mean a departure from coalition building although it would not mean a total avoidance of "politics."

The third possibility is a loosening of the connection between the military and the government, perhaps by amending the constitution to eliminate the National Security Council or to curtail its powers. The power of the president to dissolve the assembly makes this an unlikely course, but a coalition between the urban middle class officers and the middle class urban and rural groups might make this possible. It probably would matter little, since the ultimate coercive power would remain in the hands of the military, and it could return to government with little difficulty. Thus, such a change would be to a regime in which the military role on a day-to-day basis would be passive rather than active.

The development of a scenario in which the military would truly become a nonpolitical group subservient to a civilian government seems unlikely. Two previous examples might be recalled. Under Bhutto, despite the "Westminster-style" constitution, the regime became the most oppressive of all the regimes seen so far in Pakistan. He tried to limit the power of the military but ultimately failed. Zia said that it took time for him to realize the iniquities of the Bhutto period, but eventually he decided to act to purge the government of those misdeeds. The earlier example is that of the so-called parliamentary period before 1958, although, as we have noted, it was actually a period of viceregal rule which may be emulated by Zia now. Cabinets and prime ministers came and went, but the norms of responsibility of the ministry to the parliament were avoided. It is unlikely that the military would permit a return to the near chaos of that period.

Another set of scenarios deals with Islamization. It would be almost impossible for any government to propose an undoing of such Islamic law as has been introduced; it is just not in the cards to go against what is said to be the will of Allah. Retaining the present level may be the most likely future. With the defeat of the fundamentalists, further development of an Islamic state may be arrested, but what is in place will remain.

With these recent moves, Zia may well have taken his greatest gamble. Whether this has been done as the result of outside pressure, as some allege, or it was his own idea is not clear. He now must build on the groups discussed in this paper and construct coalitions of support. He has the field largely to himself. Much of the opposition to him, notably the Movement for the Restoration of Democracy (MRD), has been hoist on its own petard by its refusal to participate. Its opposition will now ring less true.

NOTES

1. David Easton, "An Approach to the Analysis of Political Systems," World Politics 9, no. 3 (April 1957).

2. Ibid.

3. Earlier reports speculated that the four provincial governors (currently military men) would also be included.

4. Christian Science Monitor, February 25, 1985.

5. The Times (London), March 1, 1985.

6. Christian Science Monitor, March 1, 1985.

Contributors

JOHN ADAMS is professor of economics at the University of Maryland. He was a Fulbright professor at Bangalore University, India, 1967–1968, and has visited the subcontinent frequently. He is the coauthor of India: the Search for Unity, Democracy and Progress and Exports, Politics and Economic Development: Pakistan, 1970–1982.

CRAIG BAXTER is professor of politics and history at Juniata College. He was a Foreign Service Officer, 1956–1980, with much of his service in or concerned with the subcontinent. His most recent books are Bangladesh, a New Nation in an Old Setting and, as editor, From Martial Law to Martial Law: Politics in the Punjab, 1919–1958.

GRANT M. FARR is associate professor and chairman of sociology at Portland State University, Oregon, where he is also coordinator of the Middle East Studies Program. He was a Fulbright lecturer in Peshawar, 1983, and conducted research on the Afghan refugees. He also lectured in Iran, 1973–1975, and was a Peace Corps volunteer in Afghanistan, 1966–1968.

RODNEY W. JONES is director, nuclear policy studies, at the Georgetown University Center for Strategic and International Studies. He also works on Southwest Asia and has extensive field experience in India and Pakistan. Recent books include Small Nuclear Forces, United States Security Policy, and Modern Weapons and Third World Powers.

CHARLES H. KENNEDY is assistant professor of political science at Wake Forest University. He has been a Fulbright scholar in Pakistan, specializing in the judicial system in that country. He has written in such publications as Asian Survey, the Journal of Commonwealth and Comparative Studies, and the Journal of South Asian and Middle Eastern Studies.

ROBERT LaPORTE, JR., is professor of public administration and director of the Institute of Public Administration at the Pennsylvania State University. His books on Pakistan include Power and Privilege: Influence and Decision Making in Pakistan, and, as coeditor with S.J. Burki, Pakistan's Development Priorities: Choices for the Future.